K.I.S.S. Parenting

Beginner's Guide for New
Parents—What Really Matters
with a Newborn

Eve Allen

© Copyright 2022 - All rights reserved.

The content contained within this book may not be reproduced, duplicated or transmitted without direct written permission from the author or the publisher.

Under no circumstances will any blame or legal responsibility be held against the publisher, or author, for any damages, reparation, or monetary loss due to the information contained within this book, either directly or indirectly.

Legal Notice:

This book is copyright protected. It is only for personal use. You cannot amend, distribute, sell, use, quote or paraphrase any part, or the content within this book, without the consent of the author or publisher.

Disclaimer Notice:

Please note the information contained within this document is for educational and entertainment purposes only. All effort has been executed to present accurate, up to date, reliable, complete information. No warranties of any kind are declared or implied. Readers acknowledge that the author is not engaged in the rendering of legal, financial, medical or professional advice. The content within this book has been derived from various sources. Please consult a licensed professional before attempting any techniques outlined in this book.

By reading this document, the reader agrees that under no circumstances is the author responsible for any losses, direct or indirect, that are incurred as a result of the use of the information contained within this document, including, but not limited to, errors, omissions, or inaccuracies.

Table of Contents

INTRODUCTION 1

NEW BABY QUICK START GUIDE 7

BABY SECTION 17

CHAPTER 1: WHAT REALLY MATTERS–DEEP BOND
....19

THE BABY'S FIRST 1,000 DAYS ARE HIGHLY INFLUENTIAL.... 20
Building a Deep Bond 23
Tell Them You Love Them 26

CHAPTER 2: ROUTINE IS YOUR FRIEND 29

ROUTINE MAKES IT EASIER FOR EVERYONE 30
Have a Loose Plan for the Day 32
Have a Laugh Along the Way 34
Build Time for You into the Routine 34
Jobs, Jobs, Jobs 37
"Do Nothing" Time with Baby 38
Creating Good Sleeping Habits 39
K.I.S.S. Checklist 41

CHAPTER 3: NUTRITION 43

BREASTFEEDING VERSUS FORMULA 43
EATING MEAT AND VEGGIES... 45
THE WAY WE EAT IS IMPORTANT....................................... 50
K.I.S.S. Checklist 51

CHAPTER 4: PLAYING IS LEARNING........................... 53

PLAYING IS LEARNING 53
ABCs or Emotional Intelligence? 54
Keep Screen Time to a Minimum 55
Encourage Moving and Nature 57

Laughing and Smiling 59
Messy Play 60
K.I.S.S. Checklist 62

CHAPTER 5: READ THEM STORIES 63

WHY READ TO YOUR BABY? 63
Ages and Stages 65
When and How to Read? 66
What to Read? 67
K.I.S.S. Checklist 68

CHAPTER 6: LET NATURE BE THEIR TEACHER 71

WHY OUTDOOR PLAY IS IMPORTANT 71
Starting Your Child's Love of Nature 73
K.I.S.S. Checklist 76

CHAPTER 7: CHILD-LED 79

WHAT IS IT? 80
Self-Autonomy 81
Is My Baby at the Right Developmental Stage? 83
Sleeping 84
Let Kids Feed Themselves as Early as Possible 87
K.I.S.S. Checklist 88

CHAPTER 8: THEY WILL COPY YOU 89

YOUR CHILDREN WILL FOLLOW YOUR EXAMPLE, NOT YOUR
ADVICE 90
What Kind of Human Do You Want to Raise? 93
Own Your Own Shit 94
Family Values 95
K.I.S.S. Checklist 95

PARENT SECTION 97

CHAPTER 9: EAT WELL 99

FOOD IS SOMETHING YOU CAN CONTROL 100
Work Toward Them Eating What You Want Them to Eat 102
Grow Your Salad Greens with Baby 103
RECIPES FOR SUCCESS 104
K.I.S.S. Checklist 106

CHAPTER 10: SLEEP WELL (AS WELL AS POSSIBLE) **107**

SLEEP MATTERS...BIG TIME 107
Have You Ever Heard of Sleep Hygiene? *110*
Where Should Baby Sleep? Your Room or Theirs? *114*
The Mythological Day Nap for Parents *115*
K.I.S.S. Checklist *116*

CHAPTER 11: GET SOME EXERCISE **119**

WHY BOTHER EXERCISING? 119
How to Pimp Your Exercise *123*
Pulling It off Can Be Tricky *123*
Modeling an Active Lifestyle From Day One *124*
K.I.S.S. Checklist *124*

**CHAPTER 12: STAY CONNECTED WITH YOUR
PEOPLE** **127**

HUMANS ARE SOCIAL BEINGS 127
Does It Take a Village? *128*
Let Others In *129*
Make the Effort to Get Out of the House *130*
K.I.S.S. Checklist *131*

CHAPTER 13: USE YOUR BRAIN **133**

WORK THAT GRAY MATTER 133
Being a Mom Is the Most Important Job in the World, But.... .... *136*
K.I.S.S. Checklist *137*

CHAPTER 14: CARVE OUT TIME FOR YOURSELF ...**139**

Fill Your Cup *139*
Anxiety Can Drain Your Cup *140*
Get Out of the House *142*
Stress Can Creep Up on Us *143*
K.I.S.S. Checklist *144*

CHAPTER 15: ACTIVELY SEARCH FOR LAUGHTER 147

IS LAUGHING OVERRATED? 148
Make Laughter Hunting Part of Your Day *149*
Do You Want Laughter to Be Part of Your Family Culture? *151*
K.I.S.S. Checklist *151*

CHAPTER 16: COMMUNICATE WELL WITH YOUR PARTNER 153

GOOD COMMUNICATION WITHIN YOUR TEAM IS CRITICAL 153
Message to Moms *154*
Message to Dads *156*
Dads Need to Get Out of the House, Too *157*
Message to Couples *157*
K.I.S.S. Checklist *159*

CONCLUSION 161

REFERENCES 167

Introduction

Nothing beats those first moments when you get to hold your new baby and stare into their little eyes. The sudden rush of mixed emotions is indescribable. You realize that you have never known true love until now and that raising this little baby is the most important thing you will ever do in your lifetime.

When taking your baby home for the first time, you suddenly lose your confidence and feel a surge of anxiety flowing through your veins. How are you going to keep this little human alive? You are now responsible for another living being 24 hours a day, seven days a week—when do I get a break again!? Oh, I don't. OMG, I don't know if I can do this.

What am I doing wrong? How do Mary and Henry make parenting look so easy? Don't worry about Mary and Henry. They have their own struggles, just like all of us. Every parent has that moment when it dawns on them that there is no baby manual. We all want to make the right decisions for our bundle of joy and each decision seems to be so crucial. Where is our elder guiding us, who has done this before? Oh crap, I don't have one. Is Google my elder? That seems a bit risky.

Having a baby for the first time can be challenging; whether you are a mom, dad, or single parent. You might have a million questions and googling doesn't help because there are four different answers to every question. Is it better to breastfeed or use formula? What if formula milk is my only option? Will my baby get enough nutrition? When will I ever sleep again? What if my motherly (or fatherly) instinct never kicks in? Why doesn't my baby sleep as well as my friend Sarah's baby? Am I doing something wrong?

As your baby gets older and more sophisticated in spitting up and sitting up, you realize they cannot live on mother's milk their whole life. The time has come for solids. Where must you begin? When will you know your bundle of joy is ready for solids? And what about allergies? It is normal to feel overwhelmed. You are not alone.

The power of raising a decent human being is in your hands. But you know what Uncle Ben said to Spiderman? "With great power comes great responsibility." You might be thinking, "Okay, Eve! You are not making me feel any better!" I want you to rest assured, you've got this. You have all the tools to be a great parent. All I am going to help you with is teaching you what each tool is used for.

My husband, Derek, and I have three children who are now five, seven, and eight, so we are just out of the other side of those intense, blurry early years. There were times when I was so sleep-deprived I felt unsafe driving. I've been high and I've been low on my parenting roller coaster, clawing my way out of depression as I got more sleep, restored my iron levels, started to see my friends again, and rebuilt my naturopathic clinic. I'm a qualified Naturopath and Nutritionist, so have had a strong focus on supporting our babies' health and well-being, learning what works and what doesn't along the way. In this book, I want to share with you the perspective we gained after years of trial and error, and more than that, research.

We have walked the baby journey for a while now and have tried all the tricks of the trade. Without any support, we figured out how to survive those early days and now we want to help all the new parents out there who might be struggling as we did. We did all the research so that you don't have to. All our research is based on recent studies and includes references.

To help you ease into your new role, we have compiled this book so that you don't have to spend hours searching the internet for answers or take all the (sometimes questionable) advice of your mother-in-law. We want to help you silence all of those voices telling you what you should and should not do. The next time Patricia suggests that you should let your baby cry it out to help them develop their lungs, you can back up your parenting choices with research. Take that Patricia!

The premise of this book is to help parents to K.I.S.S.—Keep It Simple, Stupid! This phrase was invented by Kelly Johnson, a lead engineer at Lockheed Skunk Works. She told engineers to keep their designs as simple as possible. At the time, this company designed technology that was used during the war. So, if something broke, the design should be so simple that even an amateur handyman could repair it, otherwise, it would be completely worthless during the war (Nadvinski, 2017).

This is 100% applicable to parenting. Sometimes it feels like a battlefield after being awake all night with your precious little one and the world is throwing little challenges at you. For example, your kid has a diaper explosion once you've finally packed the car and left the house, you didn't bring a change of baby clothes, your kid is screaming at you in a public restroom to sort it out, you drop your keys into the toilet and there's someone knocking at the door wanting to use the bathroom. It becomes completely overwhelming.

Now is the time to put your mama pants on and grab the keys then sanitize the shit out of your hands. That's when your K.I.S.S. training kicks in. It's simple, all you need to do is laugh it off for the ridiculous situation that it is, and get back out there. So, you strip the baby, wipe her down with toilet paper, throw her soiled pants in the trash, wrap your scarf around her waist and bust out of the bathroom with your head held high.

The other time your K.I.S.S training kicks in is when you reach a fork in the road and need to make a call on helping baby with sleeping, eating, and other milestones, and you are overwhelmed with conflicting advice from all corners. This is where you keep it simple and follow your heart after reading the research. It doesn't need to be complicated, just pick a path, back yourself, and adjust your approach later if you need to. Babies change week by week anyway-so don't sweat it, just get on with it.

Don't worry, your baby isn't as sensitive as your indoor plants (you know, if you give them too much water they die, if you give them too little water, they also die). Kids are tough and so are you. If you get the key principles outlined in this book right, then you're going to raise a good human. The nitty-gritty details of the parenting you do in the first few years will not turn your kids into dropouts or concert pianists. The most important thing you can do is to develop a strong sense of love and trust–simple right!?

You cannot spoil a baby by cuddling them, admiring their minuscule features, and feeding them when they are hungry instead of keeping to a strict schedule. My favorite piece of advice at this stage was: you're not making an end product. Who your child becomes, is not your project. You're building a safe and loving relationship. Keep this front and center. Work on teaching them what feeling love is like. This is the actual win. You will never be the perfect parent. In fact, research claims that parents get it right only about 30% of the time and still manage to raise good, securely attached children (Johnson, 2021).

Make a list of the following points and put them on your fridge. The moment you start feeling anxious, overwhelmed, or you start to doubt yourself, go and look at that list. If you are following these K.I.S.S. rules, you are doing just great! The K.I.S.S. rules are

- I look after myself so that I can be the best parent I can be.

- My number one job is to create a strong, loving connection with my baby.

- I do what feels right and ignore the advice of others.

- If it's working for my baby and it's working for me, I don't have to change a thing.

- When it stops working for either of us, that's when I seek advice.

This book is divided into two sections—the baby section, in which we discuss all things related to caring for your baby, and the parent section, where we look at some useful tips that will help you survive all those sleepless nights. So, sit back, get a cup of tea (or whatever floats your boat), and enjoy this concise yet comprehensive guide for new parents.

New Baby Quick Start Guide

When buying a new appliance, it usually comes with a quick start guide that will help you get started without any delay. This is your quick start guide for when your baby comes home. No matter how prepared you think you are, you will never be prepared for all the changes and challenges that come with a new bundle of joy.

Most new parents get swept up in all the nitty gritty gadgets available for newborns. Be careful not to fall into that trap. You don't need to go out and buy a whole lot of crap that will barely get used! Baby needs a bed, some clothes, some nappies, and the rest you can get once you know what you're dealing with such as breastfeeding or bottle feeding.

Your essentials are comfy pillows, very comfy underwear, and someone you trust to hold the baby while you shower. You'll have plenty of time to search Amazon for things to buy when you are sitting in the dark, trying to get the baby to sleep. And you will have time to go out and pick things up yourself; in fact, you'll probably love the excuse to get out of your pajamas and out of the house!

This is not a list of things that you need to buy, but rather a pep talk that will prepare you for what lies ahead.

Crying Spells

What's up with those? Keep in mind, crying is your baby's only way to communicate with you. They might be crying for various reasons–hunger, tiredness, physical touch, warmth, a dirty diaper, and in some cases, they will cry just because they feel like it. These crying spells will pass as soon as your baby understands what is going on around them. As you get to know your baby, you will start learning what their "hungry cry," "tired cry," and "cuddle cry" sound like.

Raising kids is a marathon, not a sprint. So, pace yourself if you can or you'll burn out. As adults, we cry when something is wrong. Babies, on the other hand, cry to communicate all kinds of needs. From a different perspective, a baby's cry doesn't need to be alarming. It's simply another opportunity to connect and show your baby that they are loved and cared for, which is what our role as parents effectively boils down to (Raising Children Network, n.d.).

Sleepless Nights Might Become Your New Normal

Although every baby is unique, most babies don't sleep through the night until they are at least three months old. And by sleeping through the night, I mean sleeping for six to eight-hour stretches. However, it is very normal. During those first three months, most newborns can sleep up to four hours at a time during the night. Up until the age of six months, babies' developing brains need to learn how to link the sleep cycle, which can result in many night wakings (Swanson, 2013).

But don't get too excited, usually teething starts around six months, also resulting in night wakings. But there is hope! Usually, around one to two years of age, toddlers tend to sleep better with less frequent night wakings. Toddlers might wake up at night for a variety of reasons, including separation anxiety, nightmares, illness, teething, hitting a major developmental milestone, and changes such as potty training, the arrival of a new sibling, moving, and so on. You can learn more about how to create healthy sleeping habits for your baby in Chapter 2.

Regardless of all those sleepless nights, you can find ways to get enough rest so you can survive your day! Lack of sleep can disrupt almost every aspect of your life, from putting strain on your relationship with your partner to forgetting to pack the wet wipes to accidentally giving your dog cereal and your partner dog food for breakfast! Believe me, we've been there. For the importance of sleep and some tips on improving the quality of your sleep, go check out Chapter 10.

Nutrition Is Important for Both You and Your Baby

Many say "breast is best," which is quite true in a sense. However, this is not always possible for whatever reason. There are other options available that can help you make sure your baby's nutrition is sufficient to help them thrive. For more info regarding infant nutrition, from drinking milk to starting solids, go and have a look at Chapter 3.

Nutrition shouldn't only be a priority for your little one, but for you as well. As a new parent, you are already trying to survive with minimal sleep. Don't sabotage the little energy you have left by grabbing sugary drinks, eating too much chocolate (although you might just need a little to survive), and drinking too much coffee. It is important to model healthy eating habits to your kids, not just tell them to eat their veggies! Remember, monkey see, monkey do!

Different Babies Have Different Temperaments

There are the relaxed, laid-back, "easy" babies who sleep through the night from their second week on this planet. And don't feel bad for secretly despising these babies and their parents if your baby doesn't sleep for more than 45-minute increments throughout the night. Your baby will get there; all three of our babies were terrible sleepers but they all got there in the end.

Then there are the alert, busy and cheerful babies who prefer to play rather than sleep. And all sorts of combinations of these temperaments. Get to know your baby and raise them according to their temperament, for which there are entire books available on each if interested. We generally put our kids in the "spirited" camp which comes with intensity, but also joy, and we have a shelf full of books on raising spirited kids.

Tired Cues Are Clues

Your baby has certain mannerisms that will indicate if they are either tired or overstimulated. Look out for ear pulling, yawning (obviously), and hand or finger sucking. You will get to know your baby's cues but it will take time.

Babies Aren't Manipulative and Cannot Be Spoiled

If your baby is fed, clean, and well rested and they are still crying, they might need some cuddles and comfort. Cuddle the crap out of them and give them the comfort they deserve.

Colic Is a Real Thing

What exactly is colic? Babies with colic are usually avid criers. They cry for no apparent reason. If you suspect that your baby has colic, talk to a medical professional. Maybe the doctor can offer you some advice. If that's a dead-end, try a naturopath or nutritionist who could look deeper into connections between your diet and the baby's digestive function for breastfeeding moms.

Don't underestimate the need to burp your baby, so make sure you're nailing that first if you think your baby has colic. In retrospect, we think that our kids' colic might have been caused by not burping them properly, so get on top of this skill.

Babies Usually Start Smiling Only After the First Six to Eight Weeks

Brace yourself for pouring your heart and soul into them with little reward.

Looking After Yourself Is Critical

To be the best parent you possibly can be, you need to take care of your own needs. You cannot pour from an empty cup.

Self-Care Might Take Some Extra Effort

You're going to have to work really hard to make time for yourself, such as relaxing, exercising, and socializing. These things are going to require effort, but it's totally worth it.

Try to Sleep as Often as You Can

I know it can be difficult to sleep when the baby sleeps but try at least to get some rest. The dirty floor and dishes can wait an hour or two. If day naps seem too far-fetched, but you're able to acknowledge that you need some rest, sit in a comfy chair and try reading a book. I bet you'll be snoozing after half a page and you don't have to feel guilty because, hey, you're just reading a book like a normal person.

Be Prepared to Eat Some Humble Pie

You are probably going to do all the things you thought you'd never do. For example, let your baby out of the house with food stains down their front, have the baby with a snotty nose, and be the mom in dirty pajama pants and messed-up hair.

Maintaining a Sense of Humor Is Your Secret Weapon

It gives you perspective and helps you survive hardships and negativity. But you may need to actively create the space for laughter as it can become a distant memory when you're not sleeping and plodding through the day. We've got advice on this in the Baby and Parent sections of this book.

Make Sure to Stay Connected to Your Support Network, Especially in Those Early Days

Build your support network before your baby is born. Once your baby is born, you will know who you can call if you need any help. You can connect with other new moms from a postpartum group for coffee, walking groups, church groups, exercise groups, etc. If your family is around, be honest with them about the challenges. You never know, they might just step up and help out (but don't hold your breath, just in case they don't).

If You Haven't Already, You're Going to Have Advice Thrown at You from All Directions

Approach advice like eating ribs—eat the meat but don't swallow the bones. If you don't agree or feel uncomfortable, just nod your head and ignore them. Do your research and stick with what works for you and your family.

Check In With Your Partner to Make Sure They Haven't Lost Their Sanity Through Dirty Diapers and Sleepless Nights

Before your little bundle of joy is born, be sure to work on your relationship with your partner on things like communication and teamwork. You will discover a whole new side of your partner (maybe an extra personality or two) once you both miss three days of sleep. Decide together where the baby will sleep, who will look after the baby in case of an emergency, and what to do with the baby to spend some quality time together and apart.

Communicate, Communicate, Communicate

Yes, it seems like some cliche thing a therapist would say, but it is so important to have an open channel of communication with your partner. Don't throw hints your partner's way; after all, they are probably too tired to even notice. Be clear about your expectations. And if you are unsure about something, ask. If in doubt, talk it out!

You're Probably Going to Resent Your Partner at Some Stage

Don't worry, this is completely normal. Both of you are trying to find your feet and the world is blurrier than before, so be patient with yourself and your partner.

Don't Become Rigid and Don't Micromanage Your Partner

No one likes to be bossed around and be told what to do every minute of each day. Remember that it will take a little while for you and your partner to find your groove.

Heard the Saying the Days Are Long but the Years Are Short?

This is parenting a newborn. Clawing through the day with little sleep day after day does make one wonder how long we can sustain this, but we do. Remember, this too shall pass. The only thing in life that doesn't change is that everything changes. Just when you think you're nailing it with baby, they will go and evolve to the next stage and the failproof routine you've relied on becomes obsolete. Grrrr. Well, you'll need to pull your socks up and try something new on a regular basis in order to find things that work.

You know your baby better than anyone else. Trust your gut and seek help if you need to. If you are concerned, visit a doctor, pediatrician, or nurse, even if it is only to set your mind at ease. Remember not to be too hard on yourself. You are already doing a great job by reading this book and educating yourself. You've got this!

BABY SECTION

Chapter 1:

What Really Matters–Deep

Bond

It can be very difficult to remain cool, calm, and collected while preparing for your first baby's debut. You have so much to think about: nappies, sleeping arrangements, your birth plan, the baby's room, how your pets will react, and to top it off, you are dealing with some serious pregnancy symptoms and unsolicited advice from everyone and their mother. Let's play a quick game of would you rather:

- Would you rather use cloth diapers and go insane from all the extra laundry, or use disposable nappies fearing that the eco-committee will knock on your door?

- Would you rather breastfeed in pain with bleeding nipples, or use formula milk and enrage your mother-in-law?

- Would you rather rock your baby to sleep despite your fear of doing it until your child hits puberty, or put your baby down "drowsy but awake" and miss out on all the oxytocin-inducing cuddles?

Okay, I know what you are thinking. What does *drowsy but awake* mean? And can my nipples bleed from breastfeeding? The purpose of this short exercise is to make a point. Do you think it is more important to do the "right" thing or is it more important to create a deep, loving bond with your baby? Whether you breastfeed or use formula is beside the point. You should find whatever works for you and your baby. You do you, honey. The opinions of everyone else don't matter. They are not the ones who need to keep another human being alive with minimal sleep and little to no support. If you are able to keep your little human alive and love them (despite the postpartum emotional roller coaster you are on), you have pretty much nailed it! In this chapter, we will have a look at why this deep bond is so important and how to maintain it throughout life's ups and downs. Let's get down to business!

The Baby's First 1,000 Days Are Highly Influential

The first 1,000 days of existence (from conception to a child's second birthday) have a large impact on a child's development.—
Nathan Wallis

The first 1,000 days of your baby's life set the stage for the rest of their life. As they interact with their environment, their brain is conditioned to develop in a certain way.

It is important for you to understand how serious it is to develop a deep, loving bond with your baby. They will not only feel loved and safe but, guess what? Bonding is important for optimal brain development! If your baby's physical and emotional needs are met, they are able to focus on learning new skills, playing, laughing, and doing all things baby-related. On the other hand, if these needs are not met, they go into survival mode which will activate their fight-or-flight response. To fully grasp the importance of bonding, we must have a look at some research findings—the good, the bad, and the ugly, so brace yourself!

What happens to babies if their needs are not met during the first 1,000 days of life? If infants experience excessive stress or if they are simply neglected, their brain releases high volumes of cortisol—the stress hormone. Their tiny bodies go into fight or flight mode, which can be detrimental to the development of higher brain functions. Additionally, high levels of cortisol can result in behavioral problems and stress-related diseases later in life. The best way to prevent these problems in high-risk babies is through lots and lots of physical touch together with responsiveness (Dewar, 2020) (but more on that later in this chapter).

A study done on Romanian orphans demonstrates the long-lasting effects of emotional neglect on babies. In the orphanage, babies were never picked up and held, except when they were fed, changed, or bathed. They never cried because doing so would be futile because their emotional need to be held and connected with was never met. Researchers followed these children for 14 years and found that these children's cognitive, motor, and language development were delayed. Some of these children moved to foster homes and developed quite well considering their previous neglect. However, they still showed delayed development compared to those who didn't experience emotional neglect (Weir, 2014).

Have you ever noticed how newborns fix their gaze on their mothers? This inborn tendency is very important in the bonding process. "Mutual gaze," that is, making meaningful eye contact with your baby, has been found to be linked to secure attachment, resiliency, increased concentration, and moral and rational decision-making (Ungar, 2017).

I know that the first few weeks (or even months) can be extremely hard to show that picture-perfect, Instagram-worthy motherly love to your new baby, especially if you are dealing with postpartum depression. Remember to seek professional help if you suspect that you might be suffering from postpartum depression. Maybe you haven't showered in a week, the cheese in the fridge started its own ecosystem, and let's not mention the pile of unfolded laundry. If only you could ask Alexa to fold your laundry and wash the dishes.

The challenges new mothers face seem unending, but let me tell you a little secret: what if I told you that you can feel better, bond with your baby, and release hormones that can increase overall brain development (Raising Children Network, 2022)? You can do this by simply smiling, even if you have to force yourself to do so. You can deceive your body to release dopamine and serotonin—all those feel-good happy hormones (Spector, 2018). Your baby feels secure and safe, resulting in the release of happy hormones which are vital for brain development. I'll say that is a win-win for both you and your baby! For more on laughter, go to Chapter 15.

Infants are constantly observing their caregivers' reactions to their cries for their physical and emotional needs to be met. If these needs are not being met, it may trigger genetic vulnerabilities. Research has also found that the development of a strong bond with your infant might prevent Autism Spectrum Disorder (ASD) and Attention Deficit Disorder (ADHD) in high-risk infants (Ungar, 2017).

Building a Deep Bond

In an ever-changing world, it is vital to raise resilient children. What is resilience exactly? Resilience is the ability to bounce back after facing trials and tribulations. Resilient children are confident and have excellent communication skills. They have this internal knowing that they matter and that they have an important role to play. Resilience is rooted in security and what better way to make your child feel secure than by building a deep bond with them? One-on-one time with the primary caregivers promotes resiliency. I know not everyone can become stay-at-home moms–maybe you cannot afford it financially, or maybe you would go crazy staying at home all day. No judgment here, but if you can (and want to), try to stay with your baby as long as you possibly can. If you cannot afford it or if your sanity won't allow it, don't beat yourself up.

That all being said, the question remains, how do I build a deep connection with my baby? It is simple; don't overcomplicate things. Obviously, you must tend to your child's physical needs, but by doing so in a loving, tender manner, you will instantly bond with your newborn. Make spending one-on-one time with your baby a priority. That pile of dishes calling you for the past three days can wait another three days. Do not let your chores get in the way of bonding with your baby. However, if those dirty dishes and the unfolded piles of laundry cause you anxiety, take care of them. Babies are sensitive and will sense your anxiety from a mile away.

If your baby attends daycare or stays with Grandma during the day, make sure you spend enough quality time with your baby as soon as you pick them up. To ensure that your baby develops a strong bond with their caregivers, try to limit the number of people taking care of them.

Here is a list of straightforward, uncomplicated things you can do throughout your day to bond with your baby:

- Have lots of face time with your baby. No, I'm not talking about video calling your baby at daycare (although it might not be a bad idea). I am talking about deliberately being in your baby's face, making eye contact, pulling faces, and smiling.

- Stroke your baby tenderly while changing their diaper or bathing them.

- Be responsive to your baby's cries. This lets them know that you are always there. Sometimes your baby simply needs to know that you are there. Remember, they were in your tummy for nine months, always with you and listening to your heartbeat. Now that they are born, they are exposed to a noisy, cold world, unattached to their source of comfort.

- Rock your baby and have lots and lots of skin-to-skin contact. You and your baby's bodies release oxytocin, which is also known as the bonding hormone. This might even alleviate some of your postpartum symptoms and if you are breastfeeding, it will increase your milk supply!

- Baby-wearing for the win! If you have lots of chores and errands to run, get a good quality baby wrap and wear that baby!

- Walk the walk and talk the talk. Talk with your baby in a calm, soft voice. This might be awkward at first because what will you say to a tiny human who does not understand you? You can start by talking about what you are busy with–changing their diaper, feeding them, preparing dinner, and so on. If you want to spice it up and laugh a little bit, you can sing it to them! This brings me to the next point.

- Sing! Sing anything you can think of–lullabies, songs you like, nursery rhymes, anything. You can even just hum your favorite song.

Tell Them You Love Them

Your love for your child is immeasurable. Make sure you tell them how much you love them every day. If your child grows up knowing that they are unconditionally loved, they can face anything! My parents never told me that they loved me; we never talked about emotions and that's probably how they were raised also. As a result, I was an emotionless robot for my first 20 years, as my emotions hadn't really been explored. If you grew up in a similar setting, it is time to break the cycle. Tell your children how much you love them. Yes, actions do speak louder than words, but it is important to also verbally communicate your love to them. Remember, your so-called "love language" might be completely different than your child's, so the best way to make sure they know they are loved is to talk about it with them. Telling them that you love them opens up the door to talking about feelings. Remember, monkey see, monkey do–if you open up about your feelings, your child will do the same, which will pave the way to better communication.

- K.I.S.S. Checklist

- Bonding begins the moment your child is born.

- Get the first 1,000 days right as parents and they are good to be shipped off to boarding school (just kidding).

- Skin-to-skin contact helps to build a loving bond just by cuddling.

- Gentle signing, talking, listening, and watching also help build a loving bond.

- A strong bond from early on can make your child more resilient.

- Tell baby you love them always and forever, no matter what, from early on.

- Sacrificing time to spend with your baby can come at an emotional cost for the parent. If you feel overwhelmed, ask for help.

28

Chapter 2:

Routine is Your Friend

Some days while scrolling through Pinterest or TikTok, I find myself almost gagging because every second mom posts about either their routine as a stay-at-home mom, or as they put it, a "SAHM," or their baby's naptime routine. This obsession with routines has become ridiculous, or has it? I have to admit, after having my first baby, those Instagram moms might have a point. Having a routine can be very helpful in surviving newfound motherhood, as it helps to create a flow for the day or week. Routines can foster a sense of teamwork as you go through life together. It will also help you to have a sense of purpose beyond the never-ending cycle of baby eating, sleeping, and pooping. Having a flexible routine will also be helpful in establishing healthy sleep habits for your baby. Believe me, it is most definitely worth it!

Oh, but beware of getting all OCD about your routine because some days, everything will go wrong all at once. You will spill your coffee after you realize that your baby just had a major blowout (that is code for an extreme poop explosion), at the same time your dog will use your leg as a fire hydrant and your cat will happily tear apart the neighbor's pet bird as a token of their gratitude for your hospitality, all while the smoke alarm is on for no apparent reason. The best thing to do in situations like these is to find the humor in the situation and laugh it off, but that can be easier said than done when you're sleep-deprived. Suddenly the small, insignificant things become gigantic and overwhelming.

Routine Makes It Easier for Everyone

Routine is a great way to help your baby (and yourself) feel safe and secure. Having some kind of structure in your day can help you to emotionally prepare for what lies ahead. If your child knows what happens next, the transition from one activity to the next becomes easier. This will save you a lot of blood, sweat, and tears! Every bit of energy you can conserve is gold!

Routine promotes a sense of teamwork as you and your baby navigate through the highs and lows of the day. It is important to remain flexible in your routine and celebrate the small wins throughout the day. If you rocked your baby for five minutes to go to sleep where you normally would take an hour, celebrate! If you managed to do some laundry on a particularly hectic day, do a happy dance. Make sure to acknowledge your parenting successes, no matter how insignificant they seem.

What if I told you that a well-established routine can possibly turn those "terrible twos" into "terrific twos"?

If your child knows what to expect throughout the day, they will be less likely to have complete meltdowns.

Some of the most helpful advice I have received which helped with that OCD is to make baby part of MY routine, not to change my whole life to develop a unique routine for my baby. By doing this, you can get some house chores done, run some errands, and have some me-time while the baby takes a nap.

Throughout history, and even today, many women from different cultures follow this approach. Earlier civilizations used baby-wearing as a way to protect their infants from predators. This also enabled them to gather food and get things done. Whether you are a stay-at-home mom or a working mom, others depend on you. Even to this day, women in different cultures use baby-wearing to help them get through the day. Being a mother can be extremely taxing, so it is important to use strategies to alleviate some of your anxiety. For example, Vietnamese women strapped their babies on their backs while working in the rice fields. Women in Africa and Peru still use baby-wearing today to get through the day. And a bonus is that it strengthens your attachment to your baby.

Making baby part of your routine is also a great way to give them some stability by setting an example. Believe me, you will thank me later. As soon as the baby is older, you can have them help you with the household chores, such as unpacking the plastic cutlery from the dishwasher and allowing them to "fold" your laundry.

Having a set routine might have a downside. Doing the same thing every day over and over again can feel like Groundhog Day. It might start feeling a little boring, gloomy, and robotic. When you start feeling like this, it can be helpful to plan some of those mommy-baby outings, such as mommy-and-me classes, music classes, and art classes. This will give you the opportunity to get out of the house, learn something new, and mingle with some other moms who share similar struggles. Your new mom-friends can also suggest some fun outings, or you can arrange a play date for your little ones.

Remember, babies can be quite unpredictable. They might take a while to establish a set nap routine, so it can be hard to get out of the house at certain times. It won't hurt anyone to skip your weekly mommy-and-me class. And sometimes, as soon as you think you've got it all figured out, your baby decides that it is time for a nap transition (transitioning from three naps to two, two naps to one, and so on). Don't get discouraged when this happens. It gets easier, I promise! Even though you might feel exhausted, one day you might just miss the days when you were nap-trapped with your back teeth floating (you need to take an urgent tinkle), a thirst of a thousand desert dwellers, and only Instagram or TikTok to distract you from the agony.

Have a Loose Plan for the Day

You would be surprised what a difference a simple, planned routine can make. Becoming a new mother can be overwhelming as you learn how to "read" your baby's hunger and tired cues and how to run a household while keeping your little human alive. There is very little that you can control. If you have a loose plan for the day, it can be very empowering. But, don't be fooled! Your day is most likely not going to work out as planned–they might miss their nap, have one of those famous blowouts and start crying until they eventually vomit all over your new dress, the furniture, and the dog. Don't worry, not every day will be like this. There will be days that will work out exactly as planned, where you will be able to pick up the groceries, visit the library, and reward yourself with a coffee from your favorite coffee shop. Those days are worth remembering. Some days you win, and some days you lose.

It might seem simple, but planning your day can give you a sense of purpose. Even though you might not tick off every item on your to-do list, you will still be able to get some things done. Keep it simple! Don't overcomplicate things by making a mile-long list. Having a long to-do list can be a waste of time and self-defeating unless one of the items is to screw up the to-do list and throw it away! Start with doing one or two productive things each day. Make time each morning to decide what you would like to accomplish that day. For example: "This morning we're going to focus on getting a few things done around the house, then after lunch, let's focus on outside play and do a scavenger hunt in the park, then bath, dinner, stories, and bed." If you are able to tick one thing off of your to-do list, get your child dressed and out the door in the afternoon and you can give yourself a pat on the back. And if not, good for you because you still survived the day!

Have a Laugh Along the Way

Parenthood is a journey—a challenging one! The trick is to enjoy all the ups and downs along the way by finding the humor in your situation. Sounds easy, right? But it's much harder to find the brighter side when you're sleep-deprived, barely see your friends anymore, and haven't exercised for months. Make an effort to include things in your day that bring you joy, such as podcasts, music, nature, people, animals, etc. Before you know it, you too will become one of those cringy "live, laugh, love" moms and you will love every second of it!

Build Time for You into the Routine

It is unrealistic to become one of those Pinterest moms who spend their whole day planning complex and time-consuming arts and crafts, baking, and indoor and outdoor activities. Don't get me wrong, there are some amazing tips and tricks that could help you entertain your child, but your whole day should not revolve around amusing your little one. You would go nuts! The idea is to create a balance between interactive play and independent play where you can still share the same space but both do your own thing. For example, reading a magazine with a cup of tea, having a mediocre nap on the couch, busting out some sit-ups, folding, gardening, or cooking while they learn how to play independently for short periods of time. And before you feel guilty for not spending every waking minute entertaining your little one, let's look at a few reasons why independent play is so important:

- Independent play encourages children to think outside of the box.

- It promotes problem-solving skills.

- Develops your child's creativity by encouraging them to use their imagination

- Independent play inspires curiosity and develops a love for learning.

- Offers them the opportunity to explore their emotions

- Builds self-confidence

When is the best time for independent play? Well, any time of the day will do, but it is very rewarding to do it in the morning. This will give you some time to pull yourself together. You can, for example, plan your day, have a warm cup of coffee, do some chores, or simply spend some quality time with yourself. Doing some chores or mindlessly scrolling through your phone while the baby sleeps will not fill your emotional cup.

Mindless social media scrolling can not only be addictive but can also have some negative effects on your psychological well-being. Excessive scrolling has been found to contribute to or even cause anxiety, depression, loneliness, and feelings of social isolation. Plus, seeing everyone's seemingly "perfect" lives can cause you to experience FOMO, which may negatively affect your life satisfaction and mood (Kuss & Griffiths, 2011).

Having a list of things that you can reach for when times are tough is also a good idea. Here's some homework for you; write down a list of 10 things that you can choose from to lighten the mood when shit gets hard:

- Listen to a podcast that makes you laugh.

- Play your favorite song really loud and sing along.

- Have a cup of herbal tea.

- See people you love or send them a message at least.

- Squeeze in a chapter of a good book.

- Pick some flowers from a garden.

- Take a shower.

- Brush your hair.

- Use hand cream.

- Learn a new skill.

- Cuddle your cat or play catch with your dog.

- Put on a face mask.

- Paint your nails.

- Write in your journal.

- Do some breathing exercises–there are some great apps available that you can use to show you the ropes.

- Stretch.

- Do some relaxing exercises, such as yoga.

- Make a scrapbook.

- Get a grown-up coloring book and start coloring.

- Try a new recipe.

- Put on your favorite song and dance like nobody's watching.

Jobs, Jobs, Jobs

Kiss your perfectionism goodbye when your baby arrives. Why? Because it is physically impossible to have a perfectly neat home for the first few years of parenting. When your hair is tied into a mom-bun, you have spit-up all over your clothes and you are sleep deprived, you will suddenly notice every speck of dust and one load of laundry will seem too much to handle. Just remember that it won't last forever. As you walk this new path, you will learn to adapt and develop new systems which will help you to stay sane. In the meantime, do what you can, and make peace with the temporary nature of this state of living. And stay off Pinterest. No one's home looks like that in real life.

"Do Nothing" Time with Baby

Be sure to schedule some "do nothing" time with your baby, where you simply sit and observe your baby and allow them to take the lead without any objective. Although you might get bored quite quickly, research shows that giving your baby your undivided attention can be very beneficial for them. However, there's no research about how insane parents go once the novelty of peek-a-boo wears off and you're still expected to play it for the rest of the day or until they get distracted with something else shiny or dangerous. The baby generally just wants you nearby, so even if you are lying on the ground pretending to play blocks with them when really you're passing in and out of consciousness because you're so tired, it still counts as great parenting!

Creating Good Sleeping Habits

The best weapon for establishing good sleeping habits is developing a routine. Having a routine can help train your baby's brain to know when it is time to sleep. This will also allow you to plan what you are going to do while the baby sleeps. Whether you are going to fold some laundry or have some much-needed me-time, is up to you.

Let's look at some realistic and scientific sleep expectations:

- According to the National Sleep Foundation (NSF), from birth until three months, babies are expected to sleep between 14 and 17 hours a day, 12 to 15 a day between four and eleven months, and between 11 and 14 hours a day for toddlers between one and two years (Tham et al., 2017).

- Have a look at the chart below regarding nap expectations (Dewar, 2018). Keep in mind that these can serve as a guideline, but every baby is unique. Your baby's sleep needs might be completely different. So please take these with a grain of salt and merely as a point of reference.

Age	Number of naps per day
0-2 months	3-4 naps (usually they take more naps during those first few weeks)
3-5 months	2-3 naps
6-12 months	2 naps
12-24 months	1-2 naps

Establishing a set routine for naps and bedtime will not only help your baby's brain realize it is time to sleep, but will help prevent those dreaded meltdowns or refusal to sleep. What does such a routine look like? You can start by winding them down by making sure their tummy is full, changing their diaper, reading a book or two together, and gently rocking them. You can use all these things as sleep associations—ways to tell your baby's brain and body that it is time to sleep. Other sleep aids that can be helpful are books, soft toys, or a special lullaby.

While it's risky business to depend on one book that you have to read every single night, a certain scruffy teddy that is full of milk and spit, or even a lullaby that you have learned to despise, it can be very helpful. Try to use different books, even when it is only two or three, just in case their favorite one gets lost. And as a side note—reading before bed not only calms your baby down before bed but is a great way to cuddle and connect with them. It is important to let them feel safe and loved before bedtime.

Have three spare identical teddies you can use for when one gets lost, tears, or becomes extremely dirty. And as for that dreadful lullaby, take heart, your kids won't need to hear Twinkle, Twinkle, Little Star to fall asleep when they are teenagers. Although it might seem like an eternity, this phase goes by so quickly, so just keep on doing what you need to survive.

Although you might not realize it, you too use sleep associations to help you fall asleep. It can be a skincare routine, reading a book, taking a hot shower or bath, or even drawing the curtains. Your bedtime routine helps your subconscious prepare for what is coming–glorious sleep!

K.I.S.S. Checklist

- Do something for yourself each morning and start the day on the right foot.

- Put your and your baby's needs ahead of cleaning the house. Your house won't always be this messy; it's only temporary while the baby is young. If people judge you at this stage of your family's life, then they need to get a grip.

- Dozing on the ground next to your baby playing is a totally legit parenting technique.

- Have a strategy for coping when things don't go to plan, e.g., a favorite song at the ready to blast in order to shift the energy.

- Try all sorts of bedtime routines until something works, and then stick with it. As the baby starts to figure out the sleeping thing, you can begin to do less and less of the process.

Chapter 3:

Nutrition

I am sure you have heard the famous debate between formula-feeding moms and breastfeeding moms. And the amount of mom-shaming on both sides is shocking! In this chapter, we will look at this debate from both sides. Don't worry, I am not going to bore you with endless statistics and research findings. Then, we will have a quick chat about your nutritional needs and why it is important that you take care of your own body's nutritional needs–breastfeeding or not!

Breastfeeding Versus Formula

Although the benefits of breastfeeding for both mom and baby have been thoroughly documented over many years, some mothers still choose formula over breast milk or they simply have no choice. Some benefits of breastfeeding include protecting against infectious diseases from infancy onwards, aiding in neurodevelopment, preventing asthma and allergies, and averting childhood obesity, which can later lead to chronic diseases. But it doesn't stop there, folks! Mothers also benefit from breastfeeding. It has been shown to reduce the risk of breast cancer, help your body recover after childbirth by balancing those raging hormones, aid in weight loss, and may even help prevent ovarian cancer (Allen & Hector, 2005). Plus, breastfeeding is much cheaper than formula. In fact, it is completely free!

If you are breastfeeding, keep it up for as long as you possibly can or are comfortable with it. Breastmilk is packed with everything your baby needs to thrive, and it's free (unless you're living off wagyu beef or bluefin tuna to fuel your internal milk factory).

If you choose to be a formula mom, good for you, too. There are many good-quality formulas available that will meet most of your baby's nutritional needs. Formula won't provide the probiotics essential for long-term health, though. Did you know, recent research has shown breast milk is a rich source of essential probiotics to support the long-term health of your baby, well into adulthood (Lara-Villoslada et al., 2007)? If you choose to formula feed or simply have to for whatever reason, ensure you find a quality source of probiotics intended for your baby to further protect their immune system and a multitude of other health outcomes.

There are many valid reasons why parents choose formula over breast milk. Some moms choose not to breastfeed because their babies won't latch, they suffer from chronic mastitis (painful inflammation or infection of the breast tissue), they work throughout the day and cannot find the time to express breastmilk, or they simply don't want to. Some parents or guardians simply do not have any other options, for example raising their grandchildren, being a single dad, or even being a foster parent. And that is completely fine. You choose whatever helps you survive during this transition into motherhood. Breastfeeding doesn't come easily for everyone.

Before deciding on using formula milk, it is best to discuss your options with your midwife, doctor, or nurse. They might be able to offer you some tips to help you in your breastfeeding journey, or they can suggest a specific formula that will best suit your baby's nutritional needs. Some moms choose to use a combination between breastfeeding and formula, which is also perfectly fine. Keep in mind that exclusively using formula, or combining breastfeeding and formula, will reduce your milk supply, which can be difficult to reverse.

Eating Meat and Veggies

So, when will your baby be ready to eat solids? Believe it or not, they should tell you. As soon as they start reaching out to your plate, you can slowly introduce them to solids. Now, don't spend hours preparing organic, home-cooked meals and purees because your baby will like only gum or suck on some food. You want your baby to develop a good, healthy relationship with food so don't force-feed them like a duck you would want to use to make foie gras of. Allow them to play with their food and smear it all over themselves. The mess might drive you a little bit crazy, but the sensory experience and memories they are gaining from playing with their food will have a lasting impact.

When and how can you start with solids? Babies usually show signs around six months, but it's recommended that they don't start before four months because of their immature digestive system. Signs that your baby is ready for the exciting world of solids include

- neck and head control

- the ability to sit upright with some support

- showing interest in your food

- opening their mouth when you offer them food

Your baby can start off by trying one to two teaspoons of food per day, which can be increased slowly. Remember that eating is a skill your baby needs to master. Don't get discouraged if they gag. Most parents prefer starting with smooth or finely mashed food, moving on to roughly mashed food, and finally introducing soft, chopped food. It is important to expose your baby to a variety of textures, which will encourage them to learn how to chew. Some parents prefer to spoon-feed their little ones, while others swear by baby-led weaning, but that is a debate for another day. Whichever method you choose is up to you. As long as you provide your baby with balanced meals and allow them to explore and play with their food, you are on the right track.

Research has shown that by introducing your child to food that can possibly cause allergies, you can reduce the risk of your child developing an allergy. The Australasian Society of Clinical Immunology and Allergy recommends that parents should introduce infants to common allergy-causing foods by the age of twelve months, such as eggs, peanut butter, dairy, tree nuts, soy, wheat, and seafood (Australasian Society of Clinical Immunology and Allergy, 2020). The National Health Service recommends the introduction of common allergy-causing foods by six months. Be sure to introduce only one of these foods per meal, and monitor your child closely. Look out for rashes, sneezing, runny nose, itchy, watery, or red eyes, and coughing. If you see any of these signs, contact your doctor or pediatrician immediately. If your child has no allergic reaction, you can continue to let them eat that particular food, at least twice weekly. If you continue to expose your baby to these foods, their risk of developing allergies is lowered significantly (NHS, 2020).

You don't have to become a dietician or nutritionist to start solids with your baby. Let's apply the K.I.S.S. approach here. You can't go wrong with meat and veggies; there's no need to overthink it. Don't go overboard on the dairy, because babies are snotty enough as it is, you don't need to go adding fuel to the fire. If you don't know where to start, here are some basic guidelines:

- Liver is iron-rich, which will prevent anemia and it is a powerhouse of nutrients. Sound gross? Freeze it and grate it into a veggie mash, no one will know and we can move on, nothing to see here, except a kick-ass healthy baby.

- Egg yolks are rich in omega-3 long-chain fatty acids, which are important for your baby's brain development. Fish and lightly cooked egg yolks (so as not to damage the fatty acids) from chickens fed with omega-3-rich feed provide great building blocks for your baby's brain.

- Banana is easily digested and packed with nutrients. Bananas are great as a grab-and-go food, but buy one of those banana protectors first or brace yourself for mashed banana through your handbag.

- A variety of vegetables will help your baby get used to different tastes and textures. Examples include carrots, turnips, and potatoes. Focus on complex carbohydrates, such as sweet potatoes, that will release energy slowly and take time to digest.

- Keep your precious one away from highly processed food as long as you can. If it comes in a package, question it and read the ingredients list. Not every parent has time to precook baby food and load it into reusable pouches, so if you're reaching for supermarket baby food, go for the meat and vegetable ones over the custard and fruit ones, and of course, organic is the top shelf (no chemical fertilizer or pesticides), if you can afford it.

- Do not limit your child to tasting sweet and salty food. Introduce them to sour, bitter, and astringent tastes. This will help prevent picky eating.

- It may seem obvious to many, but stick with water once your baby is weaned. I've never understood why parents introduce fruit juice aka sugar water; save it for birthday parties.

You might have a picky eater. The trick is to introduce your little one to as many healthy foods as possible from the very start. Avoid sweet treats and try not to be sneaky by hiding veggies in food. Veggies should be a normal part of your child's diet. Don't give up on giving your child healthy food. Your child needs to try a food at least 20 times before you can safely say that they don't like this or that food.

Allowing your child to eat with their hands has many benefits, including learning how to feed themselves independently, learning fine motor skills, preventing picky eating, and exploring different tastes, textures, and smells, which is important for sensory and neurological development. An added bonus is that it keeps them busy, allowing you to catch your breath. Don't stress about introducing cutlery–your little one isn't graduating finishing school soon, so take your time.

Keep in mind that your little one is constantly watching you. If you are refusing to eat the broccoli on your plate, it is likely that your baby will also refuse to eat it. Set a good example for your baby to follow.

Minimize dried fruit as it gets stuck in their teeth once they arrive. Brushing teeth is already hard enough, no need to make it harder by adding glue. This was something that caught us off-guard when adding it to lunch boxes and resulted in tooth decay.

The Way We Eat Is Important

The ultimate goal when starting solids is to get to a point where your baby is able to join you at the family dinner table. You might wonder how to get there. Easy! You make sure that the baby eats with you at the dinner table. Not only will you bond with your baby and allow them to feel part of the family, but eating together also holds many other benefits. As your baby observes you, they learn a variety of skills, such as how to use cutlery and table manners. Socializing around the dinner table promotes language development. But it doesn't stop there. The long-term benefits will positively impact your child's behavioral and academic success. Research shows that children who eat at the dinner table with their families tend to engage less in risky behavior than those who don't eat with their families. Eating together as a family is a way to establish a routine, which fosters a sense of security and belonging, which contributes to overall positive development. A study found a correlation between higher academic scores in middle and high school girls and shared family meals (Miller et al., 2012). So, can you see that involving your baby at the dinner table holds both short-term and long-term benefits?

Believe it or not, your baby will stop when they are full. You don't have to force them to eat. Once we start forcing our children to eat every single bite on their plates, they develop an unhealthy relationship with food. You can, however, introduce non-negotiable food first, such as veggies, and after they eat their veggies, you can introduce them to their favorite food, filler food (such as pasta), or other treats.

K.I.S.S. Checklist

- Fuel yourself for success. Put effort into eating well yourself, whether breastfeeding or not. That goes for dads too!

- Expose your baby to a wide variety of meats and veggies and consider staging lunch and dinner, only bringing out nutrition-empty foods like pasta once the good stuff is eaten.

- Tread carefully with processed foods. Go for the simplest meat and/or veggie version you can find (maximize nutrition and minimize sugar) and be wary of baby filling up on crackers and having no room for healthy food at meal time.

- Your baby will mimic your eating habits, so step up, eat well, and eat together as a family.

Chapter 4:

Playing is Learning

Play is the highest form of research. —Albert Einstein

We tend to underestimate the power of play. Society pressures parents to teach their children the ABCs as soon as they say their very first word. To them, I say: "no, sir! Let them play!" Research has proven time and again the importance of play in nurturing curiosity and a love for learning. Trying to be their teacher will only put unnecessary pressure on you. An ideal day for your baby's learning is probably getting messy in nature and laughing with you about it.

Playing Is Learning

Up until 18 months, physical, emotional, social, and cognitive development occurs rapidly. Whatever they learn during this period lays the foundation for the rest of their lives. As you might know already, we learn through our senses—smell, touch, sight, taste, and hearing. Playing is an ideal way of learning because your child uses all their senses to explore their environment. Your responsibility as their parent is to facilitate their learning process by providing them with opportunities to engage in free play. You don't have to make it complicated. You would be surprised what a few rocks, sticks, spoons, pots, and pans can do for your child's development. In a way, babies and toddlers can be like cats—you can buy them the most expensive, interesting, and appealing toys, and they will end up playing with the box instead of the toys!

Some benefits of play include

- promotes problem-solving, critical thinking, and reasoning skills

- teaches them interpersonal skills; such as empathy, leadership skills, active listening skills, conflict resolution, and cooperation

- develops intrapersonal skills; for example, resilience, concentration, positive self-esteem, and time management

ABCs or Emotional Intelligence?

You are responsible for laying the foundation for the rest of your child's life—no pressure! Things you can focus on as a family include self-love, self-discipline, gratitude, optimism, compassion, benevolence, authenticity, and confidence. Imagine if your child nailed these, they would most likely live a long and happy life. Isn't that what we really want for our kids? Have faith in your child's ability, sit back, and encourage them to have a go. Then reflect on what went well and what didn't go well. This will go a long way to supporting the embedding of these values and traits. And you might be tired of reading this, but your child will follow your example more than your instructions. It is important to be aware of your own stumbling blocks so that you can turn them into stepping stones. Ask yourself: Is my glass half empty or half full?

As you will see in the next chapter, educational books are highly recommended, but not for teaching them their ABCs. There are 101 other benefits of reading books with your little ones.

Keep Screen Time to a Minimum

Before my firstborn, I was adamant about not allowing any screen time because I believed that only lazy, uninvolved parents allow their children to sit in front of the television for hours on end. While this might be true, as soon as my little one became more autonomous, all those beliefs went out of the window! I never knew how thankful I would be for *Super Simple Songs* and old trustworthy *Miss Rachel.* Sometimes, a little screen time has saved my life. I could finally go to the bathroom without a baby on my hip or simply enjoy a HOT cup of tea. But do not be fooled. Screen time should not be used all the time because too much of a good thing can be quite harmful, especially for overall development.

According to research, excessive amounts of screen time are associated with low self-esteem, increased risk of mental health issues, and slowed learning (Neophytou et al., 2019). Watching hours of television has been shown to have a negative effect on a baby's eyesight, depth perception, and long-range vision. Obviously, sitting in front of a screen means less time spent talking and interacting. This can be detrimental to language development, which can cause delays in language acquisition and limited vocabulary. Studies have shown that children under three who are exposed to television, often show difficulty with concentration and problem-solving tasks compared to children who had more one-on-one interactions with adults (Day, 2020). The next piece of research might just be the cherry on top—excessive screen time has been associated with sleep issues, especially in infants and toddlers (Haughton et al., 2015).

What about those so-called educational videos designed especially for babies? If we have a look at the research, we will see that some studies claim they do not make a difference in increasing knowledge, whereas others found that they can be harmful to your child's cognitive development. In a particular study, research has shown that babies who watched *Baby Einstein* had a lower vocabulary and underdeveloped verbal skills compared to those babies who went screen-free. Who knew? Excessive screen time during infancy has been found to result in attention difficulties and reduces longer-term intelligence and creativity (Child-Psych, 2021).

Now your question might be: but should I not allow my child any screen time? Of course, you can, in fact, it might be essential to your own sanity. Below are a few tips

- Choose interactive shows that encourage singing, dancing, and mimicking.

- Watch with your child and interact with them. This will also make your bond even stronger!

- Allow 25 minutes of screen time at a time. Take a break to play or read a book. Set an alarm if you need to so that it's not accidentally an hour-long screen session.

- Don't use the television for background noise. Your child is more likely to play when the screen is turned off.

- Don't put on the TV when your child is bored—boredom is the catalyst for creativity!

- Perhaps start a new family rule that the TV doesn't go on when it's a beautiful day outside. Getting out there and enjoying it will benefit the whole family.

Encourage Moving and Nature

Children are curious creatures. To encourage them to develop a love for learning, it is important to nurture that curiosity. You can do this by putting them in settings where they can safely explore their environment.

An easy way to incorporate movement is to include it in your child's daily routine. If you can, take them swimming, sing and dance with them, roll the ball with them, push them around in the stroller, and once they start practicing walking, encourage them to push their own stroller. They love it!

You can use provocations to awaken their senses to explore their environment on a deeper level by providing them with experiences where they can freely touch, pick up, and explore a variety of objects. Provocations can be any open-ended activity or experience that encourages children to explore, be creative, and admire the world around them (Davis, 2021). Keep in mind that babies and toddlers like to put everything in their mouths. I mean everything! This is their way of learning. Be sure to keep choking hazards away. A good guideline to determine whether something is a choking hazard is to use an empty toilet paper roll. If the item can fit through the roll, it can be a choking hazard. If not, it is safe.

There is no right or wrong way to use provocations. As long as it is safe, you can use it. Provocations are usually open-ended, which means that there is no right or wrong way to use them. For example, blocks. You can do anything with blocks-build, sort by size or color, arrange from big to small, use them as toy phones, throw them, and use tongs to pick them up; the possibilities are endless. Other examples include paint, a tea set, pots and pans, fossils, magnets, sand or water play trays, and clay. Seeing mom/dad play and learn is also great for kids to see. Also, seeing mom or dad fail at things and get back up again normalizes failure and puts it into the context of an overall journey.

Laughing and Smiling

Laughter has proven to be very beneficial for our bodies and our emotional and psychological well-being. Laughter is especially valuable in the family. By using laughter to cope with very difficult situations, you teach your children resilience, moral behavior, and how to cope with disappointment, grief, or loss. It also boosts creativity and critical thinking skills (Raghuram, 2019). Laughter can be used to build a strong connection with your child (Leaps and Bounds Day Nursery, 2021), and can even be used as a discipline tool. For example, instead of getting impatient with your tantrum-throwing toddler who refuses to get in the car, make it a fun game by chasing your child to the car, pretending to be a lion wanting to eat them. Laughter can also help to heal strained relationships. Amazing!

Your best weapon as a parent is laughter! You can decide to either take life seriously and be miserable, or you can learn to find the humor in the situation and laugh it off. I have to admit that it is difficult to find something to laugh about if you haven't slept in a week, there is spit-up in your hair, your clothes reek of sour milk and sweat, and your boobs are hanging on your belly because they are stretched out from breastfeeding every two seconds and your baby just had a projectile poop all over you, the new rug, and their crib (which is three feet away). You have two options. You can have a good cry about it and while you're at it, you can use your tears to clean the floor, or you can laugh about it and wonder if anyone is going to believe you if you tell them that a two-week-old baby has the ability to spray their poop three feet away. You can even take a photo or two, just in case no one believes you. By the way, this is a true story. Believe me, I've been there! Imagine all the embarrassing stories you will be able to tell your kid when they are older!

Choosing laughter can be difficult. Sometimes, you just have to make a conscious decision to let go and laugh. First, identify your mood, admit that you are feeling overstimulated, thirsty, irritated, tired, angry, lonely, scared, sad, or needing to pee for the past few hours, and then decide what you can do about it. Right, you've identified your mood, now what? Time for something light-hearted. Try reaching for a funny book that makes you both giggle, a silly song that you can sing to, start pulling faces, or make farting sounds. No one can see you except a baby, so do what it takes to crack a smile and shake off the grump. Refer to Chapter 15 for more on laughter.

Messy Play

"Messy play" describes an integrated learning experience where children follow their own thought processes to solve problems,

exercising social, motor, and language skills through the process. The countless benefits stem from its open-endedness: the child is in charge, and there is no "right way" to play. —Kate Barber

Messy play can be something to get used to, especially if you are a clean freak. If your home is always in tip-top condition and you get upset when the pillows on the bed are the slightest bit askew, it is time to make a few changes. Children are messy little munchkins, so it is time to start practicing letting go. This free play allows them to discover their world on their own terms. Messy play can be anything from taking out all of the plastic cups and plates, smearing sweet potato puree all over the table, and squishing cut blueberries to a pulp; to slapping water, rubbing mud all over their tiny bodies, and even reaching for the dog's poop (this last one I wouldn't recommend though). Unfortunately, it's the job of a baby (once mobile) to explore and understand their world, even if it means pulling every pot out of the cupboard. Some benefits of messy play include

- promoting creativity

- allowing your child to liberally express their emotions

- developing fine motor and hand-eye coordination skills

- teaching your child to concentrate

- improving the development of social and communication skills (Barber, 2021)

K.I.S.S. Checklist

- Playing is how babies learn about the world.

- Developing emotional intelligence is more important than learning ABCs.

- Expose your baby to nature as much as possible and let nature do the teaching.

- Laughter brings benefits to kids, parents, and household vibe.

- The messier your baby gets, the happier they'll be (and the more they will learn).

- Have faith in your baby's ability; sit back and watch as much as you can.

Chapter 5:

Read Them Stories

The more that you read, the more things you will know. The more that you learn, the more places you'll go. —Dr. Seuss

Reading opens up a whole new world of endless possibilities. Why is reading to your baby so important? Well, it ticks so many boxes—one-on-one time with your baby, extra cuddles, fosters a love for reading from a very young age, aids in language development, encourages learning about new places, things, and concepts, and it becomes a normal part of your daily lives. Just picture your seven-year-old grabbing a book, getting comfy on the couch, and reading to himself. I can assure you, it's amazing! In this chapter, we will focus on the importance of reading, as well as when and how to read to your little one.

Why Read to Your Baby?

I know what you might be thinking: But my baby won't understand a word I am saying, so why must I read to them? One thing is certain: Research has proven that reading to your baby is important for brain development. It is important for developing vocabulary, listening, and memory skills, it teaches them about communication, and your baby is exposed to new information. Also, research has found that children who are read to often have a greater vocabulary by the age of two years, than those children who were never read to as babies (Lewis, 2018).

By the time your baby celebrates their first birthday, their little brain would have absorbed all the necessary sounds that are used in their native language. If you read to them often, they will hear more words and their vocabulary will expand.

Don't stick to reading only the easy words. Read the longer, more difficult words and explain to them, on their level, what the word means. You would be surprised at how much your child will understand. You might need to repeat some of the more complicated words often, but after a few times, they should be able to remember them.

Reading is also important in developing your child's social skills and increasing their emotional intelligence. As you read to them, you use a variety of sounds, facial expressions, and tone of voice to express emotions. As you interact with your baby while reading, you are encouraging them to take part by touching, pointing, and making comments along the way. As they get older, they will start to recognize some of the pictures, name them, and copy certain words and sounds.

Let's not forget how reading can help you bond with your baby. You set the example, so, if you take time to read to your baby, they will see how important reading is and will most likely develop an intense love of books.

Ages and Stages

Although your newborn will not understand a word you are saying when you read to them, their little brains are taking in every moment–building new connections with every sentence. Reading brightly-colored books with faces and patterns will teach your baby to focus. In addition to brain development, reading books and singing or reciting nursery rhymes can help to soothe your little one.

Between the ages of four to six months, your baby will show more interest in books. However, most likely not in the way you think! Instead of listening contently to your story and laughing at all the drama, your baby will start grabbing and mouthing your books. For this stage, it is helpful to use vinyl or cloth books, which will not likely tear. To lay the foundation for their vocabulary, choose books with repetitive phrases or rhyming text. Lift-the-flap books can be very engaging, but keep an eye on your baby, or they might just discover how fun it is to tear the flaps apart!

From six to twelve months, your baby will start to show interest in certain books and might even insist that you read the same story to them over and over again until, it seems, the end of time. By this age, their brains started to "click" that certain pictures represent certain things. They also start to engage, more like you would expect them to—they will start turning the pages (with your help, of course), repeating certain sounds, and pointing to pictures.

When and How to Read?

Reading to your baby is easy, cheap (free with library books), highly beneficial, and can be used as mobile entertainment when you are out and about. Most probably, you will only be able to read for a few minutes at a time and you will not finish a book. Don't be legalistic about it; make it fun. If your child likes the page with the picture of the lions, use that to your advantage. Describe the lion, make roaring sounds, discuss what the lion might be thinking, and just be creative and enjoy the time with your baby.

There is never a bad time to read to your child, but it can be helpful to make it a part of your everyday routine. In this way, you will be sure that you read to them at least once a day. An ideal time to incorporate reading into your routine is naptime and bedtime. This will not only help you to plan reading time with your little one, but will give them a chance to wind down, cuddle, and connect with you.

Reading to them at other times of the day is also important, especially when they are wide awake, alert, and ready to learn. Books are awesome boredom-busters while you have to wait, such as at the doctor's office. Be sure to keep a book or two in your diaper bag for when your little one needs some entertainment.

When reading to your little one, it won't hurt to create a little drama. In fact, they might just enjoy it. Reading should not be boring, so use your voice, make animal sounds, give each character a different voice, sing the words, and be dramatic. They love it! It is a great way to keep yourself entertained as well, but coffee or chocolate (or both) may be required for sustained periods of role-playing.

What to Read?

While your baby is still a newborn, you can read anything to them, from *Harry Potter* to *The New York Times*. At this point, they only want to hear your voice. Books with rhyming text are also recommended. As your baby gets older, they will learn how to focus on certain objects and pictures. You can then use books with simple pictures.

As they start to explore books with their hands and mouths, you can use cloth or vinyl books with brightly colored pictures of shapes, faces, and different objects. When they become more interested in what is inside the book, instead of the book itself, you can use board books that they can learn to page through. When they become more accomplished in sitting up and eating, choose books about routines, such as bath time or bedtime. As soon as your child starts talking, you can use books that repeat words, phrases, or sentences. This will help them to build on their vocabulary.

Touch-and-feel books and books with mirrors are always a winner! Photo albums are exciting additions you can use to keep them interested. Remember, your baby is not likely to sit still and listen to your story, but they will probably try to eat, page through, and even slap the books. This is all part of the process. Allow them to engage and be patient with them as they explore the exciting world of literature. Research has shown that reading to your child from a very young age will instill a love for reading, and is important for attaining important cognitive skills when they are older (Kalb & Ours, 2013).

Expose them to books as often as possible. Make sure books are available throughout the house so that they can discover them on their own. Add a book or two to their toy basket. If you get tired of your book selection, visit the library or attend baby story time events. While you're at it, set the example by choosing a book for yourself and make sure your child sees you reading often. Even if it means that you are taking a quick nap behind the book or newspaper because of your exhaustion from staying up all night with a cranky baby.

K.I.S.S. Checklist

- Cuddling while you read helps your baby feel safe, warm, and connected to you.

- Build book reading into your daily routine, perhaps nap and bedtimes.

- Reading doesn't have to be limited to bedtime. The more the better, so keep a small book or two in your bag and in the toy box.

- Choose sturdy board, vinyl, or cloth books with bright colors, textures, and repetitive or rhyming text.

- Try to make reading fun. Give animal sounds a good go, and if it's a singing book just go for it! Who cares, your baby will love it.

- Read with expression, make your voice higher or lower where it's appropriate, or use different voices for different characters.

- Don't worry about following the text exactly. Stop once in a while and ask questions or make comments on the pictures or text. ("Where's the kitty? There he is!") Your child might not be able to respond yet, but this lays the groundwork for doing so later.

- Babies love and learn from repetition, so don't be afraid of reading the same books over and over. Even if you're sick to death of the books yourself. Have a coffee and get into it!

Chapter 6:

Let Nature be Their

Teacher

In the good old days there were no televisions, tablets, or other technologically-advanced gadgets. In those days, children played in the sand, had mud baths and picnics under the trees, played with rocks and sticks, imagined pictures in the clouds, and made all sorts of concoctions out of plants and mud. The bigger the mess, the bigger the fun! Nature promotes holistic development as it stimulates all the senses. Playing in nature also makes kids healthier. Let's have a look at the importance of playing outside and how to help your child develop a love of nature.

Why Outdoor Play Is Important

Playing, whether it be indoors or outdoors, is important for your child's emotional development. Playing helps them develop their sense of self—how they see themselves, such as their characteristics, likes, dislikes, abilities, and talents. They also learn where and how they fit in the world and how the world around them works. You don't have to teach your child to play because they are designed to play. For them, play is work. Direct interactions with adults do not provide enough opportunities for children to develop social and emotional skills. It is your job to provide your child with enough opportunities for your little one to play in a stress-free environment where they are able to be creative and explore the world around them.

Nature provides children with enough opportunities to create the most exciting adventures. They are able to test their limits, practice their skills, discover their hidden abilities, and develop their self-confidence. This means that things might just get dirty, but the dirtier they become, the more fun they will have!

The outdoors also gives your child the chance to practice their gross-motor skills as they start to walk, run, skip, jump, kick, throw, and climb. This will keep them fit and healthy.

One of the greatest motivators for me to take my little one outside as much as possible is the sun. Yes, the sun! Make sure your baby doesn't get sunburned by putting on some sunscreen, wearing a hat, and staying hydrated. Being exposed to sunlight helps increase your child's vitamin D levels, which is important for healthy muscles, bones, and teeth. Being exposed to sunlight also helps your child to regulate their internal clock and boosts the production of melatonin. In simple language, spending time outdoors will help your child sleep better! For more info on how this internal clock works, see Chapter 10.

Playing outside will also help your child stay calm and relaxed, which will ultimately boost your child's mental well-being.

Starting Your Child's Love of Nature

Whenever you have the chance, take your little one outside. Being exposed to the great outdoors helps your child discover new worlds and will help them develop the self-confidence to explore. I am sure you get the point about how important nature is in your child's overall development. And now for the "how" part:

- Most parents dread "tummy time." Take a blanket or towel and practice tummy time under the trees. Your child might be so intrigued by all the leaves, they might start loving tummy time.

- Once they start crawling, you can allow them to crawl on the grass and use different props to encourage physical movement, such as outdoor furniture or boxes.

- Lie down on a blanket and watch the wind move through the trees, look at the different shapes in the clouds, and listen to the birds chirping.

- Look at the garbage truck, traffic light colors, and all the different signs.

- Smell the flowers, pick a bouquet of flowers, collect some rocks, and pick up different sizes of sticks.

- Listen to the bees, birdsong, crickets, dogs barking, horns blaring, and the wind through the trees.

- You can put them in a nature-based childcare center, or take them to parks over the weekend without a predetermined game or activity.

If you are privileged enough to have your own outdoor space, don't hesitate to take your little one outside. Be sure to keep a close eye on them as they play outside because they might just pop a bug in their mouth or take a dip in the bird bath! You know what they say: What doesn't kill you, makes you stronger!

Kids love to "help," whether it is sweeping or "folding" the laundry. Use this to your advantage by allowing them to help you work outside–pulling out weeds, sweeping, taking out the trash, hanging up the washing, or watering the garden. When your baby is still very young, you can put them in the stroller facing you as you work outside. All three of our kids used to mow the lawns on my husband's back in a sturdy baby carrier with kid ear muffs and loved it. It was a major workout for him, and if they could stay awake, they loved the noise and action. Otherwise, it was a great alternative nap routine for all involved.

An easy and low-cost option is to visit the park. This is especially helpful when you don't have a yard. It will give your child the opportunity to socialize and have enough room to run around (Raising Children Network, 2022, April 20). The park might also have some animals. Imagine how marvelous it would be to see something for the first time in real life that you have only seen in pictures. Incredible! Also, the more exposed to nature your kid is, the more likely it is that they develop a desire to protect it later in life.

Playing in nature engages all of the senses, including taste when they are really young and eating dirt! Apparently, it's good for the stomach biome if kids eat "safe dirt" (away from contaminated areas such as parking lots, sprayed areas, and so on) at a young age. It boosts your child's immunity, resulting in a healthier, happier child (Tasnim et al., 2021). You might wonder how it works. Simple: Dirt contains trillions of bacteria that are not harmful to your baby. However, because they are foreign, they stimulate your child's immune response to ward off any unwanted foreign bodies. In a way, your child's body practices fighting viruses and bacteria (Krisch, 2018).

Next time you see your baby chewing on a stick or licking the rainwater from the pavement, don't worry. Unless you have sprayed the garden or your pavement with some sort of chemical, your baby is just strengthening their body's immune response.

In an ever-increasingly digital world, it's important for kids to have good times in nature with their loved ones. Having time away from screens helps them to center, rebalance their thoughts, move their bodies, and learn about what they are physically capable of, as well as their boundaries. Imagine all the stories and adventures you can share with your family around the dinner table.

K.I.S.S. Checklist

- Get your baby outside as often as possible.

- Sun exposure equals sleep.

- Outdoor play helps babies learn about the world around them and encourages them to be more active.

- More mess often means more fun.

- Allow your baby to play with safe, natural objects like leaves and sticks.

- Put baby in a carrier while doing jobs in your yard.

- Being in natural environments can help children relax and feel calm.

- In an ever-increasingly digital world, it's important for kids to have good times in nature with their loved ones.

Chapter 7:

Child-Led

You would be surprised at how capable your little human being can be. Be careful not to get in the way by being over-protective and doing everything for them. Your job is simply to create a safe and encouraging environment full of opportunities, wrap them in enough support and self-belief, and then get out of the way! I get it, you want to protect your kid, while helping them be superhuman in every situation, but stepping back and having faith in them is one of the best things you can do for your kid long term. Even the American Psychological Association disapproves of helicopter parenting. According to their research findings, overprotective parents may have a negative impact on children's emotional well-being and behavior. These children aren't given enough room to learn how to regulate their own emotions and behavior and are more likely to act out in the classroom setting. This is because these kids are never allowed to handle emotional challenges on their own (Luna, 2018). The worst part is that helicopter parents only mean well! They just want to protect their children, but instead of helping them, they are unintentionally harming them. The quicker you learn how to let go, the better. Especially before they become teenagers. Now, that is a whole different ball game!

Provide your child with enough opportunities to choose for themselves. For example, allow them to choose between carrots or sweet potato for dinner, which book they want you to read to them at bedtime, or which ball they would like to play with.

As for the more difficult parts of parenting babies and toddlers, be sure to decide on a sleeping and potty training method that both you and your partner feel comfortable with. And stick to it! Remember, learning to sleep through the night and use the toilet takes time— it's a process. Try to enjoy the journey along the way, treasure each moment, and have a laugh about the yucky ones!

What Is It?

"Child-led" refers to the way you raise your baby. If you follow this approach, you will not try to force your baby to reach a certain milestone by drilling them, for example, potty training. Child-led means that you carefully observe your baby's signs of readiness and then create an environment for them to practice their skills. Your baby plays the most important role, taking the lead when it comes to sleeping, potty training, eating, walking, and talking. You coach or facilitate the process by offering enough opportunities that will support your child through these important developmental stages.

Don't get me wrong. You still have to help your baby take a nap, but you don't have to rock them until your arms feel like falling off and then put them down once they are fast asleep. If you do this, they are not learning the art of falling asleep and become exclusively dependent on you. The trick is to find a balance. Basically, you want to make yourself redundant so that over time you're not doing the task, your little person is. We also do not recommend the cry-it-out method, either. More on sleep below but first, let's look at some benefits of child-led development:

- Your child is more relaxed because you are not pressuring them to do something that they are not ready to do.

- You become less frustrated as you follow your child's lead.

- Your child learns on a deeper level because they are driven by their own curiosity.

- Letting your child lead in their own development helps them to develop a love for learning.

- Learning takes place more quickly because your child is interested in mastering their newfound skill (Stockdale, n.d.).

Self-Autonomy

Play is a safe way for your little one to learn self-autonomy. *Self-autonomy* can be described as the ability to act independently according to one's own values and interests (Tucker, 2014). Developing self-autonomy is important because it allows us to make healthy, informed decisions and to stand up for ourselves. You can teach your children valuable lessons by allowing them to take risks that you are comfortable with. This might sound a little bit controversial but, allowing your child to pull your cat's tail and meet the cat's claw, can save them from pulling the neighbor's dog's tail and being bitten in the face. Obviously, you should never allow or encourage your child to harm your cat or any other animal. But a harmless tug at the tail won't cause any damage. Another example is not to shout at your little one for accidentally dropping an egg. They might become fascinated by the gooey mess which will inspire them to become a world-class Michelin chef one day.

Although you should set boundaries to keep your kid safe, they can benefit from learning their own natural limits. As they get older, they will take more dangerous risks, such as climbing trees. As they climb higher and higher, try to resist the urge to tell them to be careful (although you might feel a panic attack coming on). If you encourage them along the way, they will build self-confidence and feel quite accomplished because you trusted them to make the right decisions along the way. Plus, you get to be the hero if they call for help because they got stuck. Something that motivates me to encourage good decision-making is that one day our children will become teenagers and there will be fast cars and alcohol available. Let your child take risks even if you have to bite your tongue and close your eyes. Soon you will be amazed at how far your baby has come.

Is My Baby at the Right Developmental Stage?

The biggest mistake you can make is to compare your child's development with their peers'. Just because Susan taught her little Ben to be fully potty-trained by the age of 15 months, doesn't mean you have to push your 18-month-old to use the toilet. If you start comparing your child to others, that mom guilt (or dad guilt) will start creeping up on you and you might just push your child into learning a new skill that they are not yet ready to master, resulting in conflict and insecurities.

The secret is trusting your gut, instead of looking at statistics, Susan's children, or your mother-in-law. Go with your instinct in terms of introducing the next step. If you really feel the need to teach them certain skills before they are ready, you must prepare for some hardcore battles. This will cause you and your baby to become even more stressed. If you feel like you need some guidance, find a well-experienced child development professional whose parenting style resonates with yours. This should help put your mind at ease when it comes to learning all those new skills.

One example is Kiwi neuroscientist Nathan Wallis (2020) who advises

One of the biggest risk factors facing parents is this unspoken competition that human development is a race. Development is a process, not a competition. The child that walks or talks first isn't necessarily the child that gets the best outcomes (para. 8).

Sleeping

There are so many questions surrounding infant sleep which can cause parents so much confusion and anxiety. It certainly caused a lot of stress in our family when sleep seemed to be a thing of the past. Some experts recommend cry-it-out sleep training, others suggest gentler sleep training methods, and some believe in co-sleeping or forever rocking your baby to sleep. With all of the conflicting information together with some serious sleep deprivation, it can be difficult to make a well-informed decision. We certainly tried it all out of desperation. It is completely understandable to try and find a solution to those seemingly endless sleepless nights. But unfortunately, there are no quick fixes when it comes to baby sleep solutions. We have done some serious research so that you don't have to. So, sit back, relax with a cup of warm joe, and allow me to put your mind at ease.

Every Tom, Dick, and Jane has a different opinion as to what works when it comes to infant sleep. At one end of the spectrum is the *cry-it-out* method. You start by doing the whole bedtime routine. Then you put your child down and walk away, perhaps going back in at intervals of increasing amounts of time to reassure them that you're still around. There isn't much research on the benefits of this approach for babies, but there is some research on the negative impacts, including raised cortisol levels and an increase in the fight or flight response. Excessive cortisol production is caused by high levels of stress. Sleep training has been found to increase this hormone because extreme crying spells are associated with increased cortisol levels (Dewar, 2020). This means that there is less energy available for brain development (National Scientific Council on the Developing Child, 2010). This method also causes a lot of anxiety for parents having to listen to their baby cry for hours on end. The biggest benefit of sleep training is for parents, who are able to sleep if they manage to pull it off, with their baby realizing their crying is futile.

On the other end of the spectrum is co-sleeping. Co-sleeping involves bringing your baby into bed with you. This method helps you and your baby feel close to one another, thereby strengthening your bond. Although this method is often the most convenient option, there are some downsides to co-sleeping, including the possibility of suffocation, overheating, and increased risk of Sudden Infant Death Syndrome (SIDS). A common fear among parents is that babies will become dependent on sleeping in their beds. There's an element of truth to this because of course babies would prefer to be with their parents during the night. However, sometimes it is not possible to avoid bed-sharing, especially if you take your baby out of the bassinet into bed with you to feed them. In this case, sometimes you cannot help but fall asleep with the baby in bed with you. If you create the habit of co-sleeping with your kid, you and your partner can kiss intimacy goodbye! Although we have friends who co-slept with their firstborn and they somehow managed to make another baby. They made it work somehow, so perhaps all is not lost!?

There are some safety measures you can take to avoid potential risks. Breastfeeding has been proven to reduce the risk of SIDS and is viewed as a protective measure by experts. When co-sleeping, it is important to not have any loose bedding, such as sheets, blankets, pillows, bumpers, or nursing pillows that can suffocate the baby. They should sleep on a firm mattress with a tightly fitted sheet. Do not co-sleep with others, such as other children, adults, or pets. Use a type of bolster to keep the baby from rolling off the bed and landing on the floor. And, for obvious reasons, absolutely do not sleep on a chair or the couch with your baby in your arms (Keenan, 2021).

What option is there between sleep training and co-sleeping? Easy; put your baby in their own crib and respond every time they cry. This method is not particularly popular because waking up multiple times at night can be very demanding on parents. I have to admit it did take its toll on us as parents, especially with two of them having "silent reflux" and waking up what felt like every hour. Boy! Did some coffee and dark chocolate get consumed in those days! Just keep in mind that it does get better with time. Believe me, I've walked this road with three boys. Eventually, your baby will, when they are developmentally and emotionally ready, learn how to sleep through the night. In the meantime, just remember, "this too shall pass!"

Ultimately, you should follow the approach which you are comfortable with (not anyone else; screw what your mother-in-law thinks). The important thing to remember is not to create sleeping habits that will make your life miserable in the long run. There are a variety of books, blogs, and websites on this subject, so find something that works for your family and go for it. And don't be afraid to change your approach as life changes.

Let Kids Feed Themselves as Early as Possible

Children usually start finger-feeding themselves small amounts by the age of nine months. They are usually ready to start eating with utensils between fifteen and eighteen months. Be sure to pay attention to their hunger and satiety cues. Do not force them to eat when they are showing signs of being full. You can always offer more food when they are hungry, but you cannot take the food out of their tummies when you have overfed them. Try not to give in to the urge to give one more bite. Once your toddler gets the hang of eating with a spoon or fork, allow them to eat by themselves by stepping back.

Some parents might give you the side-eye if you allow your baby to feed themselves, but keep in mind that self-feeding is important to learn about their internal hunger and full cues. They need to decide if they are hungry enough to eat, what they want to eat, and when to stop once their tummies are full. However, it's up to you to make sure that there is a high proportion of vegetables on the plate and fewer "fillers" like pasta so they don't just fill up on that. For more on nutrition, go to Chapter 3.

K.I.S.S. Checklist

- Hitting a developmental milestone by a certain age means nothing in the long term.

- This is your kid's journey. Your job is to love them, keep them safe, warm, fed, and hold a set of good values. Let them do as much of life as they are up for when they are ready.

- Figure out a sleeping strategy you and your partner are happy with. Strive to make yourself redundant. Don't be afraid to change strategies over time as the baby gets more capable of falling asleep by themselves.

- Let your child have power over things with low consequence e.g., "which book are we going to read first," "are you going to eat the broccoli or peas first?"

- Letting kids feed themselves is an easy win, but get a good drop sheet or a puppy to eat the food that ends up on the floor.

Chapter 8:

They Will Copy You

Imagine this: You are in a hurry to go to the store before it closes. In your haste, you accidentally drop a very heavy glass vase on your foot. Fortunately, the vase doesn't break, but your foot isn't so lucky. The impact of the vase is so overwhelming that you accidentally drop a swear word as the heavy object hits your foot. Because you are in a hurry, you quickly get over it, grab the car keys, a few snacks for your kid, and you plop your toddler in their car seat. As you arrive at the doctor's office, the office is extremely quiet. Suddenly, the receptionist's telephone rings and the silence is broken. Your toddler jumps up at the sound of the ringing and suddenly, very loudly, repeats the swear word you uttered earlier. Now, all, and I mean *all*, eyes are on you. How could you have taught your sweet toddler to swear like a sailor? You can be sure many parents have experienced this before. The moral of the story is, to be careful what you say or do in the presence of your toddler; they might just help you make some unforgettable (mostly embarrassing) memories.

If you haven't noticed in the previous chapters already, 80% of parenting is based on role modeling. It's worth having some awareness about what you say, how you say it, and what actions/behavior you are normalizing in the eyes of your child.

Your Children Will Follow Your Example, Not Your Advice

What does it mean that parenting is 80% modeling? Well, 80% of what your child learns comes from what they observe at home (The Parent Practice, 2020). They watch us carefully, internalizing our words, values, and actions, and then ultimately repeat what they observed from us. Holy crap, that's some pressure. Especially if you consider all the possible areas our children may be subconsciously absorbing values that we didn't intend to pass on to them.

This inborn tendency to observe our every move has the advantage of helping us grow into better human beings. Ask yourself: "If someone makes me angry, what do I do? Do I take a deep breath and speak to them rationally, or do I tend to bottle up my frustrations, or maybe explode? How do you resolve conflict, especially with your partner?" It is important to model conflict resolution skills and tell your kids when you made up after a fight.

It is important to realize that your children will learn the social skills you are modeling to them. A good way to model these skills is by allowing your children to see how you conduct yourself in social situations, for example, around the dinner table, how you interact with your friends and family, and how you talk about others. They will internalize and mimic how you talk to and treat others.

Modeling a healthy lifestyle is also important. The best way to encourage your children to eat well, exercise, drink enough water, and enjoy the little things in life is by modeling exactly that! Is your breakfast a cup of sugary coffee and do they hear that you were up half the night watching Netflix? Do you exercise with your child around, or on your own where there don't see it? Does your child ever see you reading? Your perceptions about yourself and others will impact your child's life, forever. Girls (and boys) with eating disorders usually come from homes where the parents spoke negatively about their own or their child's bodies. How do you talk to your partner about your own body shape and that of others? How you talk about others will make a lasting imprint on your child that they will carry with them into adulthood. Do you moan about your own deficiencies or make fun of others? Is your glass half empty or half full? What kind of perspective do you want your child to have?

Whatever you do becomes your child's "normal". If you smoke, it becomes normal. If you laugh it becomes normal. If you give up when things are hard it becomes normal. Is the world a kind and bountiful place, or is there a lot to complain about? Do you make healthy food choices? Is active travel something normal in your household? Is recycling just what you do in your family?

Is volunteering at your local food bank just what you do at Christmas time? Is perfection essential, or is failing okay?

When speaking about others, such as your neighbors, keep in mind to keep it real, but without badmouthing or calling them names. For example, "Oh Mike is at it again, playing his loud music. His poor eardrums, oh well, it won't last forever. Shall we go into your bedroom where it's quiet and read a story?"

What about when you are driving in the car? Does that road rage come out in front of the kids? I've heard of kids being in the car when another driver does something erratic or rude, the little kid in the back speaks up and says "asshole," and the parent is horrified. Where do you think they learned that word? From the other drivers on the road? No, kids usually learn those types of words from their parents!

Be sure not only to check their screen time, but your own as well. If you are constantly staring at the phone, your child might just ask you for one as well once they are able. When someone is speaking to you, do you stop looking at your screen and look them in the eyes? Remember, your baby is watching it all. That sounds creepy, but you know what I mean. Before you know it, your child spends more time staring at the phone than communicating with you. If your child is speaking to you, put your phone or other devices down and give them your full attention, or they might just think it is normal to talk with one another without making any eye contact whatsoever.

What Kind of Human Do You Want to Raise?

For my son's fifth birthday, we had an outdoor pizza party at our house. Someone asked me a rather deep and meaningful question. "What kind of man do you want your son to grow into?" I had recently put some bullet points into my phone to pop up and remind me of the things that I wanted to focus on for all of my three sons. So, I pulled out my list, and it felt good to have such clarity. For me they were: self-love, self-discipline, gratitude, optimism, benevolence, authenticity, problem-solving, a give-it-a-go attitude, and having a healthy start to life. Have a go at writing your own list of priorities, talk to your partner about whether they share the same views, and then let them guide you in terms of your own behavior, which of course your children are going to mimic.

Communication expert Michael Grinder once said, "The power of influence is greater than the influence of power" (Vecht, 2017, para. 9). Sometimes our children copy those things that we really don't want them to and seem to ignore those good qualities we try to reinforce. To make up for this, we can ensure that the remaining 20% of parenting is in place. This percentage consists of all the parenting tools we accumulate through experience and a little research here and there, such as setting healthy boundaries in the form of rules, setting our children up for success, motivating them to do the right thing, trying our best to understand their behavior and to respond with understanding and compassion.

Although it seems like everything you say goes into one ear and out the other, they are listening, learning, and internalizing it all. Keep on planting those seeds. You will see the fruit of your labor, even if your little tree starts to bear fruit a few years from now. Pear trees take up to six years to bear fruit, so be patient and keep on reinforcing those good values.

Own Your Own Shit

Don't be too hard on yourself. Nobody is perfect and no one expects you to be perfect. But, you do need to own your shit. Are you good at apologizing? One of the best skills you can teach your child is to fess up quickly and say sorry. It's one of those critical life skills that we all should use more often. By apologizing, you show them that you are only human, just like them, and it is okay to "lose it" sometimes. All of us feel overwhelmed at some point, especially when we are sleep deprived! If you admit your mistakes to your child, tell them what you would do differently next time (and actually do it), and sincerely apologize, you are teaching them some valuable skills that are important for life outside the safe boundaries of the home. For example, "I really raised my voice at you earlier, didn't I? It was probably quite scary and made you feel yucky. I'm sorry about that. Next time I'll try using my calm voice and dealing with my anger by stepping outside for a moment or slowly counting to five." Situations like these aren't ideal, but they can be transformed into valuable learning opportunities that your child will carry with them for the rest of their lives.

Family Values

Have you ever thought of what you would like your family's core values to be? Such as, "us Andersons really enjoy a challenge," "it's important in our family that we always care for ourselves and others," or "teamwork makes the dream work!"

Having about three main family values can be helpful. You might even choose a different value or two to focus on each month, for example, "this month we are going to focus on compassion." Start instilling these values early on, before the eye-rolling from your six-year-old begins.

K.I.S.S. Checklist

- Be the kind of person you want your kid to be.

- If you mess up, own it and talk about it.

- What does your family stand for?

- You living a healthy and happy life will increase the chances of your child doing the same.

PARENT SECTION

98

Chapter 9:

Eat Well

The urge to chug four cups of coffee (usually cold) instead of having breakfast, or stopping at McDonald's on your way home from an appointment is very tempting, especially if you have been up all night. There are very few things that you can control, particularly if you have a teeny baby to take care of. They are unpredictable, life is unpredictable, but I have good news! There is something in life that you can have absolutely all control over–what you put in your mouth. It might take some planning and discipline to kick those old habits, but once you create those healthy eating habits, you will start to feel more energized.

First and foremost, you have to look after yourself. To be the best parent you can be, you need to be strong and healthy. So, it is important for you to follow a healthy, balanced diet. Now, I am not saying you have to stop eating all your favorite treats. Believe me, there is nothing better than hitting that snack cupboard as soon as baby hits the sack! Oh, how rewarding a tub of ice cream can be after a long day of feeding, rocking, and burping your baby.

Just remember to get some balance. Allow yourself a nice treat once in a while, but does it have to be every day? Ask yourself how you actually feel afterwards. There are plenty of healthy treats out there if you're willing to do some research and try new things. Fast food, sugar, and processed foods can make you feel sluggish and irritable. Cut back on the coffee and go for some water or herbal tea instead (if you want to get your highest quality sleep). Go to sleep earlier rather than relying on coffee or sugary snacks to get you through your day.

Food Is Something You CAN Control

In an ever-changing world, there is very little that you can control. But there is one thing that you truly can control—you can have full power over what you eat and drink. If you're riding the highs and lows of a sugary diet and stimulants, then you're not going to be your best when dealing with what parenting throws at you.

Healthy eating starts at the supermarket. You are able to choose which foods you are going to buy and which you would rather avoid. Before you go to the supermarket, make sure you eat at home, even if it is a light snack. If you are hungry while doing your weekly grocery shopping, everything looks appealing, especially the unhealthy options. Oh, and the joy some comfort food brings when you have been up all night with the baby. Resist the urge to reach for those delectable chocolate chip cookies when you feel down. You might just end up in a vicious cycle: craving something salty after those cookies, then wanting something sweet again and balancing it out with another salty snack. Instead, reach for some apples or delicious berries to satisfy that sweet tooth and ward off any unnecessary cravings in the future.

Try to resist the urge to finish your baby's leftovers. Instead, you can put it in the fridge for them to finish later. This will save you some cooking time. An alternative is to get a worm farm. If you feel guilty for wasting food–the worms will love it!

If there is ever a perfect time to seek advice on nutrition, it is when you are growing a little person and when you are recovering from bringing them into the world. Be sure to seek advice on nutrition from a qualified professional, such as a nutritionist, dietitian, or naturopath.

Anemia, or iron deficiency, has been found to be a prevalent issue in obstetrics (Breymann et al., 2017). It is completely normal to have low levels of iron after giving birth. However, it can cause some serious fatigue, which does not make your sleep-deprived days any easier! Studies found that low iron levels may also contribute to postpartum depression (Wassef et al., 2018). This one caught me big time. My low iron levels didn't get picked up for a long time and I was in a deep, dark, depressed, and sleep-deprived hole for a while there.

If in doubt, go and get checked out. If you suspect your iron levels are low, get tested. Your doctor can prescribe an iron supplement. For good measure, you can always amp up your iron intake. Iron-rich foods include beef, pork, veal, chicken, fish, and certain shellfish, such as clams, oysters, and mussels. Vegetarian-friendly sources of iron include fortified cereal, rice, oatmeal, wheat, leafy green veggies (like spinach), raisins, dried apricots, and legumes, such as lentils and soybeans. Vitamin C, beta-carotene, and vitamin A help to absorb iron. So, pair iron-rich food with plenty of fruits and veggies to ensure that your body takes up enough iron to get you through your postpartum journey (Tan, 2017).

Another supplement that benefits you and your baby (if you are breastfeeding, that is) is supplementing your diet with fish oils. Studies found that women who include fish oil in their diet during lactation show higher levels of DHA in their breast milk. In other words, brain juice and an anti-inflammatory for your baby! This is especially beneficial for the brain development of premature babies. It may also lower the risk of asthma and allergies in your baby (Setterquist & Garner, n.d.).

Work Toward Them Eating What You Want Them to Eat

While it'll be a long time before your baby is eating burritos and Indian curry with you, sharing a risotto might only be a year away, and roast chicken with veggies might even be sooner!

An ideal is working toward having your kid eat what you're eating: easier for the chef and it widens their palette. According to Dr. Sarah Schenker (2021), a registered dietician and mother of two, sharing food with your baby prevents fussiness and opens up the adventurous world of different tastes and textures to your little one. No one wants that fussy school-aged kid that won't eat what's on offer at their friend's house and as soon as you show up to take them home they rush to you asking for cookies because they are hungry! The key is to ensure that mealtimes are fun, engaging, and interactive.

Grow Your Salad Greens with Baby

Teaching them about where food comes from is also fantastic. If you have the space (you only need a window sill) and a green thumb, you can involve your baby in growing some fail-proof greens. Some easy greenery to grow with kids include zucchini, beans, tomatoes, salad greens, and strawberries (Bradbury, n.d.). They can help you to water them and pull out any weeds as your baby gets more mobile. Just supervise this one or your beets will most likely also get pulled! Growing your own fruits and veggies can become a new hobby that might just help you to not go bananas (pun intended). Your little one will probably harvest your greens before they are ready, but hey, it is all about the journey, right?

Recipes for Success

Overnight Chia Seed Pudding for New Moms

This quick and easy recipe is great as an alternative breakfast or anytime snack, especially for tired new moms. It is high in fiber, protein-rich, and nutritious. You can keep the leftovers in the fridge for up to four days. So, you can also become one of those fancy Instagram meal-prepping moms without the hassle!

Prep time: 5 minutes

Ingredients:

- $\frac{1}{2}$ tsp vanilla extract
- 1 $\frac{1}{2}$ cups almond milk or water
- $\frac{1}{2}$ cup of chia seeds
- $\frac{1}{2}$ tsp ground cinnamon
- 2-3 Tbsp maple syrup
- 1 pinch of sea salt

Instructions:

1. Mix all of the ingredients together and put in a glass jar or bowl.
2. Let it sit in the fridge overnight.
3. You can serve it with berries, grated apples, bananas, nuts, coconut, cacao nibs, flaked almonds, or peanut butter to keep it interesting

4. Enjoy!

Everyday Pancakes (With Undetectable Veggies)

This recipe is a big hit for both parents and kids. You can serve this recipe in the morning, as a snack, for lunch, as a lunchbox treat, or even for dinner.

Ingredients:
- 1 Tbsp oil
- 3 eggs
- 1 tsp vanilla extract
- ½ cup milk of choice
- ½ ripe banana
- 1 medium zucchini or parsnip, cut into chunks
- 1 cup buckwheat flour (or substitute with whole wheat flour)
- 1 tsp baking powder

Instructions:
1. Preheat your frying pan over medium heat.
2. Put the eggs, milk, vanilla, banana, and veggies in a bowl and blend. You can use a stick blender or a regular blender.
3. Add the dry ingredients and mix.
4. Add the batter into an oiled and heated pan.
5. Wait until you see some bubbles, then flip it over and cook for another 2-3 minutes.

6. Before you know it, your toddler will be standing on a chair at the frying pan, asking to help flip the pancakes (and you begrudgingly say: "yes, babe," through gritted teeth, because you want them to be engaged in their food).

K.I.S.S. Checklist

- Take the time to meal plan and snack plan.

- Leave the sugary foods in the supermarket (except for chocolate; that's essential).

- Give them what you're eating when they are dabbling with solids.

- Put the leftovers in the fridge and the scraps in the worm farm (not in your mouth every day).

- Growing veggies together can be fun and educational, and save you some money!

- Think about what kind of an eater you want your child to be and model that.

Chapter 10:

Sleep Well (As Well as Possible)

One of the biggest challenges of becoming a first-time parent is sleep deprivation. If you can manage to get enough sleep, it is easy to face the world. But once you haven't slept for more than three hours in a week, life gets a little bit difficult. Suddenly, even chewing your food seems overwhelming. What if I tell you that there are steps you can take to increase the likelihood of more and better quality sleep!? For tips on baby sleep, refer to Chapter 2. For tips to improve your sleep, read on.

Sleep Matters...Big Time

The importance of a good night's rest cannot be overemphasized. Unfortunately, becoming a new parent cannot promise the luxury of some first-class shut-eye. However, if you do get the chance to take a nap or go to bed early, try to resist the urge to binge-watch your favorite show or mindlessly scroll through social media. Here's why: Research has shown time and again the detrimental effects of sleep deprivation. It may cause or contribute to a significant amount of mental and physical conditions, including

- hypertension

- mood disorders

- arrhythmia

- obesity

- type-2 diabetes

- impaired immune function

- greater risk of coronary disease

- poor memory

- lack of resilience

- glucose intolerance (Perry et al., 2013; Worley, 2018)

Not only will lack of sleep cause you to put the toilet paper in the kitchen cupboard and the coffee beans in the bathroom cabinet, but it can also cause some serious health issues that might manifest later in life. What is your approach to sleep? Do you make sure to get as much stuff done as possible so you can catch some sleep before the baby wakes up every two hours? Or are you the optimistic type who believes tonight will be different, and decide to binge-watch some shows with your significant other without going to bed early? Maybe you prefer a mixed approach—some days you are productive and responsible, and other days you decide to chill and regret it the next day.

It can be very tempting to collapse in front of the TV (oftentimes with a sleeping baby on your lap) to watch some Netflix instead of going to bed early. And it is understandable to do so, especially because you don't get to spend as much time with your partner as you did before the baby was born. However, if you are able to get into the habit of going to bed early, you might just discover that your day-to-day tasks become much easier! You may even start to find the positive in your partner again (or be attracted to them again), instead of only noticing the empty milk container back in the fridge or dirty laundry on the floor. All of this can become a big deal to someone who is sleep-deprived and has a deep source of resentment, especially if they get to leave the house every day for work and you don't! You will have more energy to get through your daily routine. It always seems like a good idea at the time to stay up late, and of course, you deserve it, but man it hurts when you've only been in bed for an hour and the baby wakes up for the first time in the night! Remember to find your balance. There is no need to stop watching your favorite show once or twice a week. After all, you need some time to reload.

If collapsing in front of the TV is the only time you get with your partner each day, then consider alternating between entertaining shows and something that might stimulate a conversation. Good examples include TED Talks, stand-up comedy, or something screen-free, such as a game of cards, planning your summer vacation, or your next renovation. Another hack is listening to podcasts together in bed, and if someone falls asleep then they probably needed it!

Ideally, you will find some time during the day to connect with your partner. Date days can be just as fun as date nights. Sometimes it means that you will have to leave the kids with a trusted neighbor or family member. A 15-minute walk around the block can be just the mini-date you need to reconnect. Having a good laugh and good sleep can fix almost anything!

Have You Ever Heard of Sleep Hygiene?

In the unlikely event of you not being able to fall asleep (due to utter exhaustion), having your own bedtime routine will help. Maybe you are one of those mythological parents who is able to get eight hours of uninterrupted sleep every night; however, you still feel like crap when you wake up. Don't worry, there are some things you can do to improve your quality of sleep that will help you wake up on the right side of the bed in the morning.

To improve your quality of sleep, it is important to understand how the circadian rhythm works. The *circadian rhythm* is a fancy word for your internal clock. This biological clock regulates your sleep/wake cycles and is programmed to work with the sun's rising and setting. As it gets dark, your body releases melatonin, which causes you to fall asleep. Approximately two to three hours after you have fallen asleep, your body slowly releases cortisol, which causes you to wake up. Cortisol secretion peaks at about nine o'clock in the morning and slowly declines during the day, preparing for the body to release melatonin so the cycle can start all over again (Bush, 2014). Now, why did you have to attend this biology lesson? To help you understand how our lifestyles have messed up our internal clocks and how to fix it! Hectic work schedules, endless screen time, and late nights all affect this natural process. Here are some tips on how you can help your body regulate its internal clock:

- Consistency is key. You can train your body to fall asleep at a certain time by going to bed at the same time every night. This will help your brain to release enough melatonin every night right before bedtime.

- Don't be shy of the sun. Exposure to daylight plays an important role in regulating your biological clock. Plus, having some fun in the sun helps your body produce vitamin D, which also plays a role in quality sleep (Muscogiuri et al., 2019).

- Focus on your bedtime routine. Use as many cues as you would like to tell your body it is time to sleep. You can take a relaxing warm shower or bath, light some candles, use fragrant body oil, read a book, drink a hot cup of herbal tea, do some stretches, or put on a chill playlist–you can use anything that helps your body relax and wind down.

- Do some exercise. Countless studies have proven the positive effects of regular, moderate exercise on the quality of sleep (Driver & Taylor, 2000). Just give yourself plenty of time to wind down between exercise and sleep if you're hitting the gym in the evenings.

- Don't drink too much coffee throughout the day! I know this one can be difficult, but too much caffeine can cause disruptions in your circadian rhythm. Your body secretes the stress hormone cortisol to wake us up in the morning. Caffeine will also interfere with your natural cortisol production, which is essential for health and well-being.

- Dim the lights and switch off those screens. Try to limit your own screen time at night and keep the lights dim. This will help your body to secrete melatonin. Remember to find that balance–it is okay to have a movie marathon now and again, but don't make a habit of it.

- Avoid drinking tea right before bedtime. This one might be a shocker, but it's for a good reason! As the sun sets, our bodies are

112

programmed to cool down internally to prepare for sleep. If you drink a hot cup of tea before bed, your body temperature rises. You are helping your body in the opposite direction (New Leaf Health Clinic, n.d.).

- Higher protein intake improves sleep quality. However, be careful not to eat too much protein right before bed because digestion slows down at night. If you like to eat a big juicy steak before bed, you might regret it in the morning, as too much protein right before bed can cause sleep disruptions (St-Onge et al., 2016).

- Histamine plays an important role in waking you up in the morning. Why am I telling you this? Because certain foods contain histamine and consumption of it at night can cause disruptions in your sleep cycle (Lin et al., 2010). Foods containing histamine include alcohol, especially red wine, fermented food, and bone broth.

- Limit alcohol intake. Yes, that glass of wine or bottle of beer might cause you to doze off but before you know it, you might just wake up in the middle of the night. Although alcohol has a sedating effect on our bodies, it also reduces the secretion of melatonin which can cause frequent night wakings.

- Drink those vitamins and minerals! Good quality magnesium and zinc supplements plus B vitamins play an important role in good quality sleep. Magnesium helps the muscles relax and B vitamins contribute to the production of melatonin which regulates your circadian rhythm and is essential for a good night's sleep (Peuhkuri et al., 2012).

Where Should Baby Sleep? Your Room or Theirs?

When our babies were tiny, we used a sidecar attached to our bed, which was great for night feeding, putting them down gently, and rolling away. It is important to take into consideration the risks of co-sleeping and room sharing. Do some additional reading to get clued in on the risks of smothering and SIDS.

As they got older (there is no magic age), we set them up with their own bed in a different bedroom. We put a mattress on the floor, getting all Montessori on it, meaning they could get themselves in and out as needed. This did result in a few midnight heart-pounding wake-ups with a toddler standing over me while I was sleeping, whispering "mom" directly into my ear. However, it did make it easier to console them when they were babies, as I could actually lie down half on their bed and half on the floor until they were settled, and then slip out the door. Pro tip: Try to get back to your bed as much as possible if you are doing any kind of sleep assistance or co-sleeping. It sucks hauling yourself out of their warm bed to trudge down the hallway back to your bed, only to be called for again

114

in another 20 minutes. But if you do not make a habit of co-sleeping, they are used to sleeping in their bed and you regain your bedroom for the grown-ups only. Believe me, it's blissful not having a little snorter in the room. For more info on co-sleeping and the effects of sleep training, refer back to Chapter 7.

The Mythological Day Nap for Parents

I am sure your grandma thought she gave you a golden nugget of advice right before your baby was born—sleep when the baby sleeps. Oh, of course, Grandma! I will magically fall asleep in unison with my baby while driving the car or at the dinner table in the middle of the conversation. While we're on the subject, will the baby also do laundry while I do the laundry? Or wash the dishes while I wash the dishes? While some parents benefit from this advice, we never managed to nap during the day. Many parents use the baby's naptime as an opportunity to get things done.

It is important to note that daytime naps can be very beneficial for your health and overall emotional well-being. People in the corporate world who choose to indulge in a quick nap during the day have proven to have higher levels of performance compared to those who don't nap during the day. It improves your emotional state (Dhand & Sohal, 2007) and can help with memory retention (Ficca et al., 2010). You would be surprised at how many iconic people were (or still are) serious nappers in their day. Winston Churchill was the one who invented the term *power nap*. He believed that naps were necessary to get through the day. Doctor Strange, Benedict Cumberbatch, is an advocate for napping when the baby naps. He believes that it is the only way to remain sane in his newfound fatherhood. Gwyneth Paltrow seems to love taking naps, as she has designated nap areas throughout her home (Burke, 2020). Albert Einstein loved his sleep. He would sleep for long stretches at night and take a nap or two for good measure during the day (Moraligil, 2021). Although daytime naps might be a bit tricky, it is certainly worth it–these famous people can testify! If you find it difficult to take a nap during the day, do something relaxing, or even boring. Put on a YouTube video of someone peeling an egg (yes, people do that!) or building a pool in the forest, and soon you might find yourself dozing off to blissful sleep. And don't listen to that inner voice judging you; after all, you are educating yourself.

K.I.S.S. Checklist

- Going to bed early some nights is something you can control and will feel better for.

- Try and find time to connect with your partner child-free during the day sometimes.

- There's sleep and then there's deep sleep. Hopefully, you get some of the latter and take the steps you can to increase your chances.

- Come up with a sleep strategy for the baby together as it will deeply impact you both and you will need the support of each other no matter what pathway you take.

Chapter 11:

Get Some Exercise

Exercise gives you more energy. What!? Yes, it might seem contradictory, but it really works. You might wonder how you can scrape together enough energy to exercise when you are barely getting through the day. No one is expecting you to become the next world-famous bodybuilder. Exercise doesn't necessarily mean that you need to go to the gym for hours on end. Just make a few lifestyle changes and you're good to go! In this chapter, we will look at the importance of exercise and how to incorporate it into your daily routine.

Why Bother Exercising?

As you know by now, exercising on a regular basis sets a good example for your kids. However, there are many other benefits of exercising that can help you get through this challenging journey of parenthood.

Before you can incorporate exercise into your routine, it is important to recover from giving birth. This does not mean that you are not allowed to exercise. On the contrary, light exercise can help you recover faster, even after a traumatic birth experience. Be careful not to engage in strenuous exercise if you had a complicated birth experience until your health professional gives you the all-clear. The whole idea is not to exercise to drop a pound or two of the baby weight (although it would definitely be welcome), but help your body and mind recover. Exercise during the postpartum period has been proven to help alleviate postpartum depression symptoms. Remember, your hormones are going crazy after giving birth, which may cause some baby blues. Feelings of depression and anxiety are completely normal during this period. If you feel overwhelmed, be sure to speak to a medical professional.

Exercise during this time helps your body recover from the grueling birth process—whether you gave birth vaginally or were a c-section mom. It helps to strengthen the muscles and tighten the skin. Contrary to beliefs and old wives' tales, science has shown that mild to moderate exercise will not cause your milk to become sour or dry up as long as you stay hydrated (Mottola, 2002). And believe me, you will keep your water nearby because there is no thirst as intense as a breastfeeding moms in the middle of the night! It is wise to keep in mind not to overdo exercise while breastfeeding, because it may cause some accumulation of lactic acid in the breast milk. Exercise increases oxytocin levels which is important for bonding with your little one (Yüksel et al., 2019). A little more on oxytocin later.

Start small—take a brisk walk, even if it is only for a few minutes. Slowly increase your speed and time as your body adapts to your new routine. Keep the following guidelines in mind (especially if you are breastfeeding):

- Do not engage in strenuous exercise, such as training for the next body-building convention or climbing Mount Kilimanjaro.

- It is best to exercise right after feeding your baby.

- Drink enough water before, during, and after exercise.

- Don't worry about dieting. Make sure you eat enough nutritious calories to fuel your workout, produce enough milk, and recover.

- Avoid tight sports bras. Rather wear a high-quality bra.

- Make sure you are taking in enough calcium and vitamin B6, preferably through food, but use high-quality supplements if needed (Mottola, 2002).

Let's not stop with moms. Dads, grandparents, and foster parents can also benefit greatly from regular exercise. But don't you need the energy to work out in the first place? Well, yes, but you've got to start somewhere. Exercise increases all those feel-good hormones, including serotonin, endorphins, and dopamine. I am sure you want to play ball and run around with your own grandkids one day. How?

Exercise! It strengthens muscles (obviously), is good for your heart health, and increases bone density.

Let's get back to oxytocin. Studies have shown that new fathers also undergo some hormonal changes—they also secrete oxytocin, the bonding hormone. Where women's bodies produce this hormone during birth, skin-to-skin contact, and breastfeeding, men's bodies produce oxytocin when they play with their babies (Emory Health Sciences, 2017). Women naturally respond to their babies' cries in the middle of the night, thanks to this hormone. Oxytocin does not have the same effect on men—it reduces testosterone that causes aggressive behavior and increases bonding with their newborn and partner. So, ladies, don't get angry if your partner seems to ignore your little one's cries in the middle of the night. They physically are not preprogrammed to respond as quickly as you!

The point I want to make is that fathers can benefit from exercise and they should use the production of oxytocin to their advantage—play with your baby! Play can be a fun form of exercise. Strap them to your body and do some lunges, mow the lawn, or take them hiking. You can even squat and lift them up in the air, Lion King style. Hakuna Matata!

Doing exercise tends to lead to other good decisions, such as good food choices and going to bed earlier. Next thing you know, you've got yourself a healthy lifestyle on the go!

You only need to do some moderate exercise for 15 minutes per day. We can find room for that, can't we? To get maximum benefits, bust this out well before or right after your baby's nap time so that you can involve your baby in your exercise regime (assuming you're working out at home, pushing a baby stroller at high speeds, or attending a baby-friendly class). By exercising during your baby's awake time, you also avoid having to fit exercise in during their nap time, freeing you up for other things. Ideally, you'd do something that gets you as sweaty as possible, because it will trigger more physical and mental health benefits.

How to Pimp Your Exercise

To get the most out of your workout, go outside. Getting some sunshine also holds some amazing health benefits. Or recruit a friend to join you. You can share the horror stories of parenthood or brag about how little sleep you got the previous night. Even better–get some exercise with a friend, in nature! This way, you can reload and take some time to reflect on your fast-paced urban life. If you don't have any mom (or dad) friends, see if you can join a local parenting group that will motivate you.

Pulling It off Can Be Tricky

It can be difficult to get some exercise in, especially if there aren't any eager grandparents nearby to babysit. Where there is a will, there is a way! You can start off by taking turns with your partner. This will give you an excuse to kick your partner off of the couch when it is their turn!

You could try doing a swap with another mom or a group of moms. For example, three moms rotate taking turns—two get to go for a power walk in nature together, while the third looks after the kids at their house. Alternatively, you can strap your baby to your body and go for a walk, and you will get some bonus resistance training in the process. The bouncing will probably send the baby off to sleep if well-timed.

Modeling an Active Lifestyle From Day One

Model an active lifestyle for your baby if you can bring them along somehow. There are plenty of exercise classes around now that welcome having little ones crawling around, so look around. "Being active is just what we do in this family."

Investing in a good stroller is probably worth it if it enables you to get out and push bubs along the footpath at high speeds. This was the only way we could get our firstborn son to sleep. Man did we rack up some miles, come rain, hail, or shine.

K.I.S.S. Checklist

- Make time for exercising; it will make you feel better.

- Exercise usually leads to other healthy choices, such as better nutrition and sleep habits.

- If possible, exercise with others and in nature to maximize the benefits.

- Be careful not to push yourself too soon after childbirth. It's better to build up slowly back into your kick-ass self!

- It's worth leaning on friends and family to make exercise happen.

- Make having an active lifestyle part of the family culture.

126

Chapter 12:

Stay Connected with Your

People

We are not made to become hermit crabs, hiding in our shells, bearing our own burdens, and living solitary lives. We need each other to survive, especially parenthood. Although it might seem like too much trouble to go out with friends once in a while, it is definitely worth it for your own sanity and to be the best parent you can be. I am sure you have heard of that analogy about self-care–when on a plane, you, the adult, should first put on your oxygen mask when things go wrong, before helping others. Filling your emotional bucket works the same way. You cannot keep another human alive if your tank is empty. You don't have to do this whole parenting thing alone. Find your tribe to improve your parenting vibe!

Humans Are Social Beings

We were created to seek help from the community. In ancient societies, women initially did not receive any help in taking care of and raising their children. During these times, fertility rates were low and they lost many children. As time went on, mothers started relying more on others to help them raise their children, including older siblings, neighbors, grandmothers, and other relatives. Naturally, this resulted in higher fertility rates and decreased infant morbidity (Kramer, 2011). If this doesn't convince you to seek some social support, I don't know what will!

Today's world makes us more isolated than ever before. These days, families are living in all parts of the world and people do not know their neighbors' names. Having a sense of community around you can be highly supportive and get you through some dark times. Just because it's commonplace, you do not have to struggle through a baby's early years alone. It is not only good for you to seek help from those around you, but your baby can also benefit from coming into contact with others often.

Does It Take a Village?

What does "it takes a village" mean? We are in charge of the very early days of our babies' lives and can shelter them from all of the impurities in the world for a while. However, it doesn't take long for other influences to come in, and by then you're probably ready to hand your kid over to trusted people in your life (or complete strangers if you're tired and over it!). If you retain a strong bond with your kid, they will most likely take on your moral code, which will serve them well in the crazy old world we live in. As an added bonus, community involvement can be beneficial to your child's social and emotional development. Being part of a community helps you and your child feel that they belong, your baby is exposed to a new learning environment, they learn from an early age to rely on others if they need help, and it enhances language development (Raising Children Network, 2022, December 19).

Let Others In

It's natural to want to protect your precious little bundle from the world and not leave her with anyone else. But letting go a little and handing the baby over to those you trust, so you can put on some nice clothes or hit the gym, will probably do your mental health a lot of good.

Allow close friends and relatives to take over for a while, even if they irritate you with their unsolicited advice and stereotypical views on gender roles, such as girls being delicate creatures having tea parties in pristine white dresses, and boys being cowboys who don't cry. Although it might be difficult to let go, your child needs to be exposed to all kinds of views. You can discuss these opinions with them when they are old enough. In the meantime, go fill your cup, even if it means you have to bite your tongue every time grandma mentions how your little boy should toughen up or how your little lady should not be allowed to play with cars.

Make the Effort to Get Out of the House

If you have joined a prenatal group, mommy-and-me class, or postpartum support group, it can be helpful to meet with them often to discuss your struggles and learn some new tips and tricks from other parents. Just be careful of comparing your baby's developmental milestones with other parents' babies. Just because Susan's baby started crawling at six months, doesn't mean your baby should do the same. Or even worse, maybe her little bundle of joy sleeps through the night by two weeks. It doesn't mean you are doing something wrong with your kid for waking up a gazillion times a night. Your prenatal nurse or pediatrician usually does a short interview with you to determine if your baby is on track. So, don't compare, because there is likely nothing to be concerned about. Every baby is on their own journey and if you're taking the time to read this book, then your baby will grow up just fine at the end of the day. It means nothing that your baby isn't gurgling or rolling onto her tummy yet!

If you have workmates who you actually want to see— great, take the baby in for a visit. If you're into taking your baby out with your friends, then great. If your friends aren't in the same stage of life, hang out with them, but also try and find some people in the same boat as you. For example, groups that involve some sitting down together like music shows, church, etc.

Trying to put on a friendly face in front of strangers might be the last thing you feel like doing after weeks, or even months, of little sleep. But getting out of the house and sharing the odd story about the highs and lows of new parenting can be helpful in seeing that you are not the only one, and others also have their own unique challenges. It can be so relieving to hear that others are struggling, too. There's definitely a wicked part of me who indulges in hearing the hardships of other parents, helping me remember that every family has their crap they're dealing with.

If your parents suck in terms of offering to look after the baby while you get some sanity, or they're not around, find surrogates or pay someone if you can afford it. Getting a babysitter for a couple of hours during the daytime is also a great idea if the family budget can afford it (cancel one of your TV subscriptions to make this happen!). Going for a child-free walk through the park with your partner can be so uplifting!

K.I.S.S. Checklist

- Make the effort to get out of the house, ideally without a baby sometimes!

- Trusting others to look after your baby can be tricky for some parents, but worth giving a go.

- Retaining old friendships is important, as is connecting with other new parents.

- Set yourself a goal of a number of social outings per week, if that helps motivate you.

- Taking turns to stay home with your baby is a winner (as long as it's balanced), but try to create opportunities to get out of the house baby-free together whenever possible!

Chapter 13:

Use Your Brain

Being a stay-at-home parent can be an ungrateful job, and it might feel like your brain cells are dying. You do the same things week after week without some kind of reward; no pat on the back, no "good job, Doris," no work incentive, no nothing. Just poopy diapers, messy meals, and endless laundry. Or, maybe you are a working parent, which can be just as challenging. Waking up early to get as much done as possible before heading off to work, missing your baby, driving home during peak traffic, coming home, preparing dinner, and doing the bedtime routine with your little one. Every day becomes one big blur and let's not talk about the mom (or dad) guilt. Using those marvelous brain cells while baby is still young can help you gain more confidence, and might even help you adjust to work life once your maternity (or paternity) leave is over.

Work That Gray Matter

It's common to feel like you're on a hamster wheel, doing the same thing each day, playing baby games, reading baby books, and let's not forget the endless renditions of Old McDonald Had a Farm. It's therefore important that you make time to use your brain. Whether it be reading a page of your favorite book each night before you pass out exhausted, or you find a word game you like, such as Wordle, that you can do while you're having your morning coffee. Just do something that will help you get those brain cells working. And learning new things makes us feel good! Apparently, we get a dopamine hit when we learn new things or accomplish challenging tasks, making us want to achieve more, onwards and upwards (energy levels permitting)!

As you might know, your brain consists of a right hemisphere and a left hemisphere. Each side has an important role to play. The left side is responsible for logical and analytical thinking, whereas the right side is responsible for subjective, intuitive, and creative thinking. Although you might tend towards one or the other, in reality, both sides of your brain work together. Science shows us that the brain works best when both sides are stimulated (Sparling, 2015).

To activate the left side of your brain, you can do the following

- Do some puzzles, such as sudoku, crossword puzzles, or scavenger hunts.

- Work those brain cells by solving some brain teasers.

- Learn a new language.

- Read a fiction novel.

The right side of the brain can be activated through

- painting or sketching.

- pottery.

- learning to play a new musical instrument.

- listening to new music.

- meditation (Hill, 2022).

Use a combination of these activities to make sure both of your brain hemispheres are activated. Work these activities into your daily routine as best you can and you'll be killing it. To strengthen the connection between your right and left brain, you can do some midline exercises. In these exercises, you cross both sides of your body. For example, while stretching, you can touch your right foot (if you can bend that far) with your left hand and vice versa. Here are some other ideas:

- Hand-clapping games with your little one (Pat-A-Cake is always a winner).

- Play some tennis or baseball.

- Put your dancing shoes on.

- Play ball with your little one or your furry child (DeYoung, 2020).

Being a Mom Is the Most Important Job in the World, But...

Raising a little human is possibly the single most important thing you'll ever do. But if you're up for it, having a side project can be good for giving you a sense of purpose beyond wiping bums and trying to get the baby to sleep all of the time. Some project ideas could be

- Learn a language.

- Create or maintain a garden.

- Write a blog.

- Work your way through a series of podcasts.

- Create a side hustle.

- Do some small house renovations while your baby is asleep.

- Volunteer at an animal shelter.

- Do a handful of hours of work at your old job each week.

The trick is to not bite off more than you can chew. The last thing you want to do is add stress to your life. The point is to mix it up in terms of your headspace, use different parts of your brain, and have something other than babies to talk about as you jazz up your social life again.

K.I.S.S. Checklist

- Include word or number games into your daily routine.

- Find something creative to do that's fun and make space for it.

- Reading fiction is a great way to escape while using your brain.

- Consider a side project to work on, but keep it low-stress.

- Using our brains makes us feel good.

Chapter 14:

Carve Out Time for

Yourself

You don't have to spend all of your time gazing at your little miracle with stars in your eyes. It is okay to take some time for yourself. In fact, if you do this, you will feel cooler, calm, and collected, and will therefore be a more patient parent for your little one.

Fill Your Cup

You cannot pour from an empty cup. Sounds familiar? Unfortunately, or instead, fortunately, it is true. Taking time to do something you enjoy can help you become the best parent you can be. I am not talking about the so-called self-care of taking a quick shower or buying groceries without the baby, or taking extra long on the toilet so you can scroll through Instagram. I would call this escaping to take a breath. I am referring to taking some time to do something you really love, such as attending a cooking class, going for a hike, having alone time to read in peace, hanging out with friends, or doing whatever makes you happy.

If you don't know where to start, make a list of all the things you enjoy doing every day or week. What is "your thing"? Are you the nature-lover who loves mountain biking, or the indoor type that loves to get all cozy on the couch with a good book? Try to think of those things that bring you joy and rank your list from one to ten. Come up with a plan of action to integrate your top three in your week, or if possible, every day. It can be helpful to do this exercise with your partner so that you can plan your time and support one another.

If you feel overwhelmed or anxious about your little one not getting the sleeping memo, keep in mind that the vast majority of other parents have the same struggle and that there are things you can try, but ultimately it's your baby's journey and you are merely the support person. Yes, your little night waker might be the reason you feel tired, which can contribute to feeling overwhelmed. However, there is something you can do before those feelings of defeat grow into uncontrollable monsters.

Anxiety Can Drain Your Cup

In the past, parents did not experience as much anxiety as we do today. Why? Because in the past, children were economic assets that helped their parents on the farm or with the family business. In today's day and age, children don't contribute to the household's income. Except for those notorious parents who use their kids to make millions on YouTube or TikTok. Today, we as parents pour all of our financial, emotional, and physical resources and energy into our children, and for good reason—we want them to become responsible, successful adults. What makes it even harder is the fact that the world is changing so quickly with the expansion of technology, the availability of contradicting information, changing politics, and a significant increase in world crises. We cannot predict which specific skills they will need in the future.

In addition to these stresses, couples are trying to figure out their roles as new parents. Many women today are working moms who are trying to juggle their responsibilities at home and at work. Non-traditional families are also improvising as they go along. These new roles as parents can cause a lot of strain on relationships. Resentment is common for most couples as they are trying to navigate these new responsibilities. Ladies, who asked their man to look after the baby while you fold the laundry or cook dinner? Suddenly, they need to use the bathroom. And the best part is, by the time they are done, you could have cooked a three-course dinner!

Along with all the uncertainty, changing roles, and relationship conflict, parents all have one goal in common—raising kids who are happy and protecting them from this unstable, cruel world. Yes, we all want our kids to be happy, but it is an unfair burden to place on yourself as a parent. It is even more unfair to expect your child to be happy all the time. We place so much pressure on ourselves, that we forget the most important thing—simply to love our children and teach them the difference between right and wrong. Happiness and self-confidence would automatically be a byproduct of feeling loved and learning how to do good unto others (Senior, 2014). So don't empty your cup by worrying about what tomorrow will bring or placing pressure on yourself to make your kid smile all the time.

Get Out of the House

It is important to have other things going on, other than raising little humans. Let me remind you of the previous chapter—use that gray matter! Activating both hemispheres includes socializing, seeing new places, and trying new things. This might sound far-fetched, but if you focus all of your attention on your baby, you might just end up resenting them or wishing your time together would fly by so that life could get back to "normal" again. Guess what? It won't! Children have a way of changing your life as nothing else can!

So, how do you manage to go to that yoga class with baby? You don't. If you have a family member who can look after your little one for a few hours a week, allow them to help you. If not, you and your partner can take turns looking after the baby. This will allow each parent to put some special "me time" aside for themselves.

And when that "mom guilt" comes creeping up on you, remember, "distance makes the heart grow fonder." If getting out of the house seems too far-fetched or causes you too much anxiety, start small—go buy milk at the grocery store while your partner takes care of the baby, go for a 15-minute walk, or just go to a different room and have your morning coffee in silence while staring out the window. Want to take your coffee hit to the next level? List 5 things that you are grateful for. Some say gratitude is the key to happiness. While it takes skill to find the silver lining in some situations, those who do it by reflex are served well.

Stress Can Creep Up on Us

Stress can be very, very sneaky. It creeps up slowly and before you know it, you are having a complete meltdown. Believe me, been there, done that, got the T-shirt. When we stress, our bodies release the stress hormone cortisol. The long-term effects of cortisol production can be detrimental to our health. Don't get me wrong; our bodies need cortisol because it has anti-inflammatory properties, turns glucose in our bodies into energy, helps us wake up in the morning, and helps us to integrate fear-inducing memories for future survival. However, chronic production of cortisol due to stress has been associated with cortisol dysfunction and increased pain, anxiety, depression, and inflammation (Hannibal & Bishop, 2014). Other side effects of high cortisol levels include an increase in weight, skin problems including acne, a decrease in muscle strength, fatigue, irritability, high blood pressure, headaches, impaired concentration, and a tendency to bruise easily (Santos-Longhurst, 2018).

Our bodies need time to calm down and repair after we experience high levels of stress. When you become a parent, you can't just take a sabbatical from parenthood to recover from life's stresses. You will have to actively choose to take time for yourself to recover; it won't happen automatically. Monitor your stress at least once a month. Set a reminder on your phone if necessary. Just start somewhere. So, find your thing and preferably something out of the house, whether it be exercise, guided meditation classes, attending a pottery class, coffee with a friend, or a slow walk in nature, and build it into your week. Journaling or blogging can also be highly therapeutic to processing and dealing with all those overwhelming thoughts and feelings of parenthood.

K.I.S.S. Checklist

- Be 100% clear on what brings you joy.

- Writing down how you feel can be a great way to get it off your chest.

- Plan ahead to build "me time" into your day or week.

- Be disciplined and uncompromising in doing your thing(s) daily or weekly.

- Set a reminder on your phone to check your stress levels once a month.

- Distance makes the heart grow fonder, so get out of the house!

Chapter 15:

Actively Search for

Laughter

Laughing might be the last thing you want to do, especially if you have been up at midnight for the past week with a tiny, teething human who suddenly wants to learn how to crawl. It might be something that feels like a distant memory, something you used to do before baby, but it's worth actively targeting today for a bunch of reasons. Laughing makes us happier, healthier, and more pleasant human beings. There aren't any pills in the world that can bust stress and depression as well as a good, hearty laugh. The trick is making it something that naturally occurs; easier said than done when recovering from birth or you're sleep-deprived. You can't force yourself to laugh, but you can create the environment for laughter to occur and then let go a little, relax, and see what happens. If you suspect that depression might be creeping in, be sure to seek help from a trained professional. For more on why laughter is beneficial for your kids, refer back to Chapter 4.

Is Laughing Overrated?

Laughing can help you not to take life too seriously and face the day, even if you have missed your morning coffee. Believe me, you will need some humor in your life if you have to scoop poop out of the bath for the umpteenth time. Laughter is not only necessary for your own sanity, but is actually good for your health, relationships, and overall well-being. It is great to help you cope with stress, releases endorphins (feel-good hormones), and reduces high blood pressure (BabySparks, 2018).

As you might know, laughing is like yawning—contagious! If your little man or little lady sees you rolling on the floor with laughter, you can be sure that they will want to join in the fun. Laughter is so much more than making primitive, sometimes animalistic, and snorting sounds. When you laugh at someone's joke, you are communicating to them that you understand them, you enjoy their company, and, in some cases, that you love them. Studies have shown that couples who deal with difficult situations through laughter report higher levels of satisfaction in their relationship, and they tend to stay together for longer (Scott, 2015). If you and your partner can manage to laugh together, you will be able to get through some tough times together, and might even end up on the other side, stronger together than ever. In the next chapter, we will have a closer look at how to strengthen your bond with your partner through communication.

Make Laughter Hunting Part of Your Day

It sucks to be at this point in life, but sometimes you just have to get off your butt and find laughter, even if your situation doesn't seem all that funny looking through exhausted eyes.

Look for opportunities to laugh. Some ideas include

- Like the "Fill Your Cup" section, it might be helpful to write a list of all the things that make you and your partner laugh. Find a way to integrate them into your day or week. I wish we never got to this point and laughter just came naturally all the time. But hey, let's get real, it doesn't, so let's grab the bull by the horns here!

- My husband is a real asshole; he starts crying with laughter when watching people hurt themselves on *Funniest Fails* The more they get hurt, the more he laughs. Next thing I'm laughing my face off at him. This stuff is contagious, so give some thought to what makes your partner crack up, too.

- Look at yourself—if you are still a fresh parent, just looking in the mirror at that messy mom-bun can be enough to laugh about. In your mind, you might look like an Instagram-worthy new mother, but in reality, you look like Miss Trunchbull from *Matilda*.

- Look at your situation—maybe your happy place is now being alone on the toilet.

- Attend a stand-up comedy show—this one is the perfect idea for a date night.

- Do some laughter yoga—this probably won't happen, but they say it is good for you.

- Watch a comedy on Netflix—you might just fall asleep, but it is worth a try!

- A little fake laughter goes a long way—one day, while having a laugh with one of my boys, I decided to add a little bit of extra fake laughter. Before I knew it, he was laughing harder than before. I found myself laughing even more because he was laughing more.

- Schedule a comic date night with your significant other—schedule a specific night each week to watch a stand-up comedy show (if getting a babysitter isn't practical, watch a movie that will make you and your partner laugh).

- Call your funniest friend—we all have that one friend that knows exactly how to make us laugh. Make a point to phone that friend or organize a coffee date, if possible, at least once a month.

- Get a little silly by starting a water fight with a friend the next time you visit the local pool.

- Create a Pinterest board of things you find funny, such as memes.

- Listen to a funny podcast during the day.

- Once you discover the things that make you laugh, do more of them!

Do You Want Laughter to Be Part of Your Family Culture?

This might sound like a broken record, but remember to model joy and happiness to your children. Laughter can be contagious, especially if it is part of the family culture. Laughing about the mishaps, misfortunes, and misadventures can turn almost any situation around. Before you know it, the big things become the small things and you are able to cope better with life's lemons. However, you have to consciously choose joy, which can be very challenging when you have slept only four hours in two days.

K.I.S.S. Checklist

- For more on why laughter is beneficial for your kids, refer back to Chapter 4.

- Write a list of all of the things that make you laugh, and build them into your day or week.

- Seek things that make your partner laugh. Remember, laughing is contagious, so you benefit, too.

- A happy family is a healthy family (and visa versa).

Chapter 16:

Communicate Well with Your Partner

Think your relationship is airtight and bulletproof? Have a baby! There is nothing like exhaustion to trigger all those hidden, mostly insignificant, issues in your relationship. Whether it is the way your partner chews their food or how they leave the toilet seat up, having a new baby can bring out the worst (and best) of us. The only way to survive this is through teamwork. You know what they say: "teamwork makes the dream work." Yes, it might sound a little cliché, but it's true. In this chapter, we will have a closer look at how to communicate better with your partner to survive those early days of parenthood.

Good Communication Within Your Team Is Critical

Without good communication skills, your team is doomed. A helpful tool to improve your communication with your partner is to do the Five Love Languages program (Chapman, n.d.). This program will help you understand yourself and your partner better and will improve your communication skills. Even if you think you've got this, when sleep deprivation kicks in, rules of engagement change, and shit can get hard. So, watch out for the early signs of miscommunication, and see if you can get your partner on board to talk about what's going on. Bringing things up like the fact that communication isn't working can be tricky and uncomfortable. However, if you are able to convince your partner to read this chapter or to watch a communication-related TED Talk together, it can help improve your relationship in a non-confrontational way.

Message to Moms

Ladies, men are not as complicated as you might think. They need you to give it to them straight. They don't even notice when you drop hints here and there. It's not their fault, it is just the way they are wired. This can be quite frustrating to you because you have no idea why your man won't pick up on your hints and you end up resenting them.

When my husband got super tired, he would go quiet, turn into an emotionless robot, and plod through the chores until collapsing in bed. It used to drive me nuts when I would want to debrief about my uneventful day and he would barely acknowledge me, or I'd be angry at him about something and would only get a monotone response. It took me a long while to accept that going into "battery saver" mode was his coping mechanism.

Men can get overwhelmed, too, they just show it in different ways. Try to be as gentle and as supportive as possible, and make your expectations clear. Instead of telling your partner that you are thirsty, ask them directly if they would mind making you a cup of tea. Instead of leaving all his clothes on "the chair" (you know, that chair where you put all your clothes that are too clean to wash and too dirty or wrinkly to wear?), ask him to throw his dirty clothes in the laundry and pack away his clean clothes.

Your partner is definitely going to have a few mishaps, such as putting the diaper on backward, causing it to leak, which means more laundry for you. Yay! Think your partner sucks with the baby? Ask around and you might find that actually, you scored a pretty good sucker to raise kids with. Don't be too hard on him; he is doing his best. After all, you are the boss so don't be a mean one. No one likes a meanie. Be a good employer by giving him clear instructions and being quick to forgive. Ideally, try to find the humor in the situation and laugh it off. It might not seem that way, but you are going to look back at those memories and laugh at all the unfortunate adventures you had with your partner. We even write a few of the funny ones down so that we can remember and laugh at them later. A team motto that got us through some dark times was similar to the Emergency Management motto for surviving natural disasters, "just get through," and we did ride out the storm alive and together.

Message to Dads

For the dads out there: If in doubt, just communicate. Your partner is unlikely to ever say, "you're giving me too much information about what you are thinking, feeling, or planning on doing next." I'm not sure that any woman has ever said that to a man in the history of the world. So try it for a week and see what happens. Do your best to shake off the grump from being tired, and share information with your teammate:

- Would it be helpful if I stayed out longer with the baby to give you some more space at home, or is that going to mess up the routine?

- Let's write a list of household jobs and put our names by the ones that we are responsible for, just so it's super clear who is doing what.

- I'm thinking I might stay behind at work for a beer today because we have just closed that big deal, would that impact you and Baby?

Ask with genuine interest how your partner's day has been over dinner, even if it's highly likely that the structure of their day was exactly the same as the day before. There will always be highs and lows amongst them that your partner will probably like to talk through with someone on the inside who actually gets the grind, without having to sugarcoat things.

Don't expect your baby mama to carry the load of researching the various opinions for each fork in the road and make all of the baby-related decisions. Do your own research so that you can also bring suggestions to the table and take some of the weight off your partner.

Dads Need to Get Out of the House, Too

Sometimes, being a dad can be freaking hard, often juggling a different set of balls than the mom. Men can sometimes bottle up stress until it surfaces negatively in one form or another, so make sure you're releasing the pressure valve regularly. Checking in with your dad-buddies to see if they also find parenting tough can be good sometimes, but if it's not the sort of thing you talk to your pals about, then there is probably a local men's group you can join and hear the stories of others as well as share your own. Some men struggle to talk about their emotions, so find your outlet and build it into your week. My husband used to treasure his bike ride to and from work to clear his head, having the odd beer with his friends, and going hiking periodically to escape it all.

Message to Couples

If you're messaging each other on your phones when side by side on the couch, it's time to reassess and change things up. If you can maintain good communication during the hard years of having little children, then your relationship is much more likely to make it out the other side, and might even bring you closer—what a thing to share!

Those who play together stay together, but don't pressure your partner into sex. They might just need more sleep and to get out of their tracksuit to feel sexy. Men, the last thing your lady might think about is being touched, especially in an intimate way. Remember, she has little hands all over her the whole day; pulling her hair, sucking her boobs dry, touching her face, poking all her sensitive bits, and sitting on her lap while she pees. She might just need some time to herself before you start caressing her thigh. It also helps to let her vent a bit about her boring (or horrific) day. If you're nailing the communication thing, you're more likely to get laid.

Ladies, believe me, it is very difficult to accept your man's affection after a long lay of "momming," but you still need some physical affection from your partner. You might not feel like it, but if you allow your man to give you a long, tight hug, just breathe and wait for those happy hormones to be released. You will feel more relaxed and connected. Some experts say that intimacy drops away when couples stop touching each other. Touching produces oxytocin (a love chemical). So, remember to lie in each other's arms when watching movies, or try a massage swap if you think communication and intimacy could be improved. If you guys can raise little people together, you can achieve anything!

158

K.I.S.S. Checklist

- Discuss the importance of good communication with your partner but remember that it can be really challenging when exhausted.

- Set a reminder on your phones to check in with each other on how things are going.

- Moms, be forgiving of the dads who put in the effort.

- Dads, if in doubt, just communicate, even if you don't feel like it.

- Keep the touching up, but it doesn't have to be sexual.

Conclusion

Parenting is hard because children aren't born with an instruction manual. Even though parenting can be difficult, it doesn't have to be complicated. The first 1,000 days are the most important. Work on that heart-to-heart connection by spending time with your baby, cuddling them, laughing with them, telling them how much you love them, playing with them, and just spending as much quality time with them as possible. If you've nailed this part, you're pretty much an amazing parent.

Developing a flexible routine can be very helpful, even though you won't be able to stick to it most days. Remember to work some me-time into your routine. Remember, to be the best parent you can possibly be, you need to look after yourself first. You don't have to entertain your little one all the time. Allow them to get bored; it's good for them (and for you, too!). They work on their independence and problem-solving skills, while you can sit back, relax, and take a breather!

Both breastfed and formula-fed babies turn out just fine. Use whatever works best for you and your family. However, speak with your healthcare professional before you decide on formula milk so that they can talk you through the things to consider. Remember that once you start integrating formula milk, your own milk supply might be impacted.

And don't skimp on a nutritious, balanced diet for yourself. You are responsible for laying the foundation for your child's future eating habits. Start modeling healthy eating habits from the beginning. Don't worry, you don't have to give up your guilty pleasure. Some chocolate now and again ain't hurt nobody! On the contrary; dark times call for drastic measures—eat that cake, drink that wine, and have a feast once in a while. Moderation is key!

Don't give in to the milestone police. If Susan asks you if Junior is sitting up yet or if he took his first steps yet, ignore her. All happens in good time. Don't become anxious and rush your baby; keep your own insecurities out of it! Focus on building that connection and let them play! After all, for your little one, learning is still all fun and games. Let them get dirty. Believe me, you will quickly overcome your perfectionism once your baby starts eating solids and playing in the mud. And don't rush your baby to the hospital if they ate a handful of soil. A little bit of dirt goes a long way (for their immune systems, that is).

If you want a smart and worldly kid, read with your baby and read in front of your baby. Set an example for them and they will develop a love of reading. Their future language teacher will thank you one day if you start teaching them the value of reading from infancy.

Be sure to take your baby outside as much as possible. The benefits of playing outdoors are endless–from practicing their skills to improved sleep (which is my greatest motivator. Mama needs her sleep!).

Decide what kind of human you would like to raise and become that person yourself. Your kid will not do what you say, they will do what you do. Don't just talk the talk, remember to walk the walk! If you make a mistake, say sorry. If your child sees that you are also a human that makes mistakes, they will realize that you aren't perfect either and that it is perfectly okay to make mistakes.

Even though your whole life revolves around your baby's needs and well-being, you should remember to take care of yourself by eating a healthy diet, exercising, trying to get as much sleep as you possibly can, and working on your relationships. Find some hobbies you enjoy. You need to stimulate those marvelous brain cells, or you just might lose them! Hanging out with other interesting grownups helps you retain your confidence in life and keep your small troubles in perspective. So, make time in your week somehow and get out there.

Find your support network. Find other parents that you can share your challenges with. You might just realize that what you are experiencing is entirely normal. Join an exercise or church group, do an occasional babysitting swap, take a walk, or go for a coffee with other parents. Build your support system. Allow your mother-in-law to help out now and again so you can get some space. But be prepared for lots of unwelcome comments or advice. Just let it roll off like water on a duck's back. Did your partner turn out 100% perfect? No, so she's no more qualified than you. Your survival and sanity are worth more than debating some minor issue.

Laugh at the mishaps. The greatest parenting mistakes often become the best memories. Sometimes, you just have to let it go, lighten the mood with a joke about the situation, and shake it off with a laugh. To do this, you sometimes need to force yourself to laugh. Look for the humor in the situation. You are in control of your feelings, so take charge and laugh it off. Whether you want a home of grump or a home of joy, the choice is yours!

Focusing on good communication between you and your partner is worth its weight in gold. Some relationships don't make it through those early years. Poor communication is sometimes to blame and we don't want that to happen to you guys! Ladies, don't beat around the bush. Tell your man what you need. I promise you, they are more likely to support you if you spell it out for them. Gentlemen, if in doubt, communicate. Ask questions, and make sure you know what your partner expects of you. Do the Five Love Languages test. You might just be surprised at what small things you can do for your partner that will let them know how much you care about them. It can be something as small as taking out the trash without being asked, making your partner a cup of tea, leaving a love note on their pillow, or even touching their shoulder as you walk past them. It is the little things that count.

You know what they say, "the days are long but the years are short." Before you know it, baby will be walking, talking, and off to school! There is so much conflicting advice out there, I hope you find the confidence to do it your way with laughter and love. If in doubt, don't overthink it, just keep it simple, stupid!

References

Allbritton, J. (2001, December 31). *Feeding babies.* The Weston A. Price Foundation. https://www.westonaprice.org/health-topics/childrens-health/feeding-babies/#gsc.tab=0

Allen, J., & Hector, D. (2005). Benefits of breastfeeding. *NSW Public Health Bulletin, 16*(3-4), 42-46. https://www.phrp.com.au/wp-content/uploads/2014/10/NB05011.pdf

Applied Social Psychology. (2019, March 16). *Mindless scrolling.* Pennsylvania State University. https://sites.psu.edu/aspsy/2019/03/16/mindless-scrolling/

Australasian Society of Clinical Immunology and Allergy. (2020, November). *How to introduce solid foods to babies for allergy prevention—Frequently asked questions (FAQ).* https://www.allergy.org.au/patients/allergy-prevention/ascia-how-to-introduce-solid-foods-to-babies

BabySparks. (2018, April 6). *Developmental benefits of humor.*

https://babysparks.com/2018/04/06/develop
mental-benefits-of-humor/

Barber, K. (2021, November 25). *Why children need messy play.* Family Times. https://familytimes.co.nz/children-need-messy-play/

Boyle, A. (2013, June 13). *This is your brain on fatherhood: Dads experience hormonal changes too, research shows.* NBC News. https://www.nbcnews.com/sciencemain/your-brain-fatherhood-dads-experience-hormonal-changes-too-research-shows-6C10333109

Bradbury, K. (n.d.). *Fruit and veg for kids to grow.* BBC Good Food. https://www.bbcgoodfood.com/howto/guide/easy-crops-kids-grow

Breymann, C., Honegger, C., Hösli, I., & Surbek, D. (2017). Diagnosis and treatment of iron-deficiency anaemia in pregnancy and postpartum. *Archives of Gynecology and Obstetrics, 296*(6), 1229–1234. https://doi.org/10.1007/s00404-017-4526-2

Burke, C. (2020, June 9). *Napping with the rich and famous: Top eight most famous nappers.* Sleep Advisor. https://www.sleepadvisor.org/famous-nappers/

Bush, B. (2014). *The role of cortisol in sleep.* Natural Medicine Journal. https://www.naturalmedicinejournal.com/jour nal/role-cortisol-sleep

Chapman, G. (n.d.). *Discover your love language.* The 5 Love Languages®. https://5lovelanguages.com/

Child-Psych. (2021, September 18). *Do baby educational videos work?* https://www.child-psych.org/do-baby-einstein-dvds-work-exposing-infants-to-educational-dvds-may-affect-their-language-development/

Cuddlebug. (2018, June 15). *Baby wearing around the world in different cultures.* https://www.cuddlebug.co/blogs/news/baby-wearing-around-the-world-in-different-cultures

Davis, E. (2021, January 27). *Learning through provocations: Why learning provocations make for inquisitive children.* Famly. https://www.famly.co/blog/learning-through-provocations

Day, L. (n.d.). *Screen time for babies and children.* Baby Sensory. https://www.babysensory.com/content/S6372 73919256091946/Screen%20Time%20for%20 Babies%20and%20Children.pdf

Dent, M. (n.d.). *Play and nature play.* Maggie Dent. https://www.maggiedent.com/common-concerns/play-nature-play/

Dewar, G. (2018, May 2). *What's normal? An evidence-based baby sleep chart.* Parenting Science. https://parentingscience.com/baby-sleep-chart/

Dewar, G. (2020, February 2). *Stress in babies: How to keep babies calm, happy, and emotionally healthy.* Parenting Science. https://parentingscience.com/stress-in-babies/#:~:text=If%20babies%20are%20expos ed%20to

DeYoung, K. (2020, May 15). *40 crossing midline activities you can do at home!* OT Perspective. https://otperspective.com/40-crossing-midline-activities-you-can-do-at-home/

Dhand, R., & Sohal, H. (2007). Good sleep, bad sleep! The role of daytime naps in healthy adults. *Current Opinion in Internal Medicine, 6*(1), 91–94. https://doi.org/10.1097/01.mcp.0000245703.9 2311.d0

Driver, H. S., & Taylor, S. R. (2000). Exercise and sleep. *Sleep Medicine Reviews, 4*(4), 387–402. https://doi.org/10.1053/smrv.2000.0110

Emory Health Sciences. (2017, February 17). *How dads bond with toddlers: Brain scans link oxytocin to paternal nurturing: Study looks at neural mechanisms of paternal caregiving.* Science Daily. https://www.sciencedaily.com/releases/2017/0 2/170217095925.htm

Ficca, G., Axelsson, J., Mollicone, D. J., Muto, V., & Vitiello, M. V. (2010). Naps, cognition and performance. *Sleep Medicine Reviews, 14*(4), 249–258. https://doi.org/10.1016/j.smrv.2009.09.005

Gavin, M. L. (2021, January 14). *Toddlers at the table: avoiding power struggles (for parents).* KidsHealth. https://kidshealth.org/en/parents/toddler-meals.html

Greene, M. F. (2020, June 23). *Thirty years ago, Romania deprived thousands of babies of human contact.* The Atlantic. https://www.theatlantic.com/magazine/archive /2020/07/can-an-unloved-child-learn-to-love/612253/

Gross, S. M., Shapiro, J. F., & Gabriella Terhes Karlsson. (2021). *The simplest baby book in the world : you got this! : the illustrated, grab-and-do guide for a healthy, happy baby.* Simplest Company.

Halim, S. (2019, June 19). *Parent and child exercise: the importance of exercising as a new parent.* Health Europa. https://www.healtheuropa.com/parent-and-child-exercise/92058/

Hannibal, K. E., & Bishop, M. D. (2014). Chronic stress, cortisol dysfunction, and pain: a psychoneuroendocrine rationale for stress management in pain rehabilitation. *Physical Therapy, 94*(12), 1816–1825. https://doi.org/10.2522/ptj.20130597

Haughton, C., Aiken, M., & Cheevers, C. (2015). Cyber Babies: The Impact of Emerging Technology on the Developing Infant. *Journal of Psychology Research, 5*(9). https://doi.org/10.17265/2159-5542/2015.09.002

Hill, S. (2022, July 27). *Left vs. right side of the brain.* Healium. https://www.tryhealium.com/2022/07/27/left-brain-vs-right-brain/

Johns Hopkins Medicine. (n.d.). *Sleep/wake cycles.* https://www.hopkinsmedicine.org/health/conditions-and-diseases/sleepwake-cycles

Johnson, P. (2021, August 6). *Good enough parenting.* Forest for the Trees Perinatal Psychology. https://forestpsychology.com.au/good-enough-parenting/

Kalb, G. R. J., & Ours, J. C. van. (2013). Reading to young children: A head-start in life? *SSRN Electronic Journal, 40.* https://doi.org/10.2139/ssrn.2267795

Keenan, R. C. (2021, November 18). *Experts have finally acknowledged how common co-sleeping is, despite all the warnings*. Today's Parent. https://www.todaysparent.com/baby/baby-sleep/safe-co-sleeping-according-to-experts/

Kramer, K. L. (2011). The evolution of human parental care and recruitment of juvenile help. *Trends in Ecology & Evolution, 26*(10), 533–540. https://doi.org/10.1016/j.tree.2011.06.002

Krisch, J. (2018, June 11). *Just let your kids eat dirt. It's good for them*. Fatherly. https://www.fatherly.com/health-science/let-kids-eat-dirt-gut-health

Kuss, D. J., & Griffiths, M. D. (2011). Online social networking and addiction--a review of the psychological literature. *International Journal of Environmental Research and Public Health, 8*(9), 3528–3552. https://doi.org/10.3390/ijerph8093528

Lara-Villoslada, F., Olivares, M., Sierra, S., Miguel Rodríguez, J., Boza, J., & Xaus, J. (2007). Beneficial effects of probiotic bacteria isolated from breast milk. *British Journal of Nutrition, 98*(S1), S96–S100. https://doi.org/10.1017/s0007114507832910

Leaps & Bounds Day Nursery. (2021, September 30). *The importance of laughter for little ones*.

https://www.leapsandboundscc.co/importance-of-laughter-early-years/

Levy, A. S. (2019, March 15). *Why independent play is vital for raising empowered children.* Family Education. https://www.familyeducation.com/active-play/why-independent-play-is-vital-for-raising-empowered-children

Lewis, K. N. (2018). *Reading books to babies (for parents).* KidsHealth. https://kidshealth.org/en/parents/reading-babies.html

Lin, J.-S., Sergeeva, O. A., & Haas, H. L. (2010). Histamine H3 receptors and sleep-wake regulation. *Journal of Pharmacology and Experimental Therapeutics, 336*(1), 17–23. https://doi.org/10.1124/jpet.110.170134

Luna, K. (2018, June 18). *Helicopter parenting may negatively affect children's emotional well-being, behavior.* American Psychological Association. https://www.apa.org/news/press/releases/2018/06/helicopter-parenting

Miller, D. P., Waldfogel, J., & Han, W.-J. (2012). Family meals and child academic and behavioral outcomes. *Child Development, 83*(6), 2104–2120. https://doi.org/10.1111/j.1467-8624.2012.01825.x

Ministry of Education. (2019, February 20). *Learning through play – What's it all about?* https://nzcurriculum.tki.org.nz/Curriculum-resources/NZC-Online-blog/Learning-through-play-What-s-it-all-about

Mireault, G., Sparrow, J., Poutre, M., Perdue, B., & Macke, L. (2012). Infant humor perception from 3- to 6-months and attachment at one year. *Infant Behavior and Development, 35*(4), 797–802. https://doi.org/10.1016/j.infbeh.2012.07.018

Moraligil, N. (2021, October 5). *Famous people who loved to nap.* Meditopia Blog. https://blog.meditopia.com/en/famous-people-who-loved-to-nap/

Mottola, M. F. (2002). Exercise in the Postpartum Period. *Current Sports Medicine Reports, 1*(6), 362–368. https://doi.org/10.1249/00149619-200212000-00010

Muscogiuri, G., Barrea, L., Scannapieco, M., Di Somma, C., Scacchi, M., Aimaretti, G., Savastano, S., Colao, A., & Marzullo, P. (2019). The lullaby of the sun: the role of vitamin D in sleep disturbance. *Sleep Medicine, 54*, 262–265. https://doi.org/10.1016/j.sleep.2018.10.033

Nadvinski, M. (2017, February 24). *KISS is an acronym for "Keep it simple, stupid" as a design principle noted by the U.S. Navy in 1960.* LinkedIn https://www.linkedin.com/pulse/kiss-acronym-keep-simple-stupid-design-principle-noted-na%C4%91vinski

National Scientific Council on the Developing Child. (2010). *Stress and the Developing Brain.* Center for Early Childhood Mental Health Consultation. https://www.ecmhc.org/tutorials/trauma/mod2_3.html

Neophytou, E., Manwell, L. A., & Eikelboom, R. (2019). Effects of excessive screen time on neurodevelopment, learning, memory, mental health, and neurodegeneration: a scoping review. *International Journal of Mental Health and Addiction,* *19*(3). https://doi.org/10.1007/s11469-019-00182-2

New Leaf Health Clinic. (n.d.). *Sleeeeepp.* https://www.newleafhealthclinic.co.nz/blog-2/sleeeeeppp

NHS. (2020, December 7). *Food allergies in babies and young children.* https://www.nhs.uk/conditions/baby/weaning-and-feeding/food-allergies-in-babies-and-young-children/

Perry, G. S., Patil, S. P., & Presley-Cantrell, L. R. (2013). Raising Awareness of Sleep as a Healthy Behavior. *Preventing Chronic Disease, 10*(133). https://doi.org/10.5888/pcd10.130081

Peuhkuri, K., Sihvola, N., & Korpela, R. (2012). Dietary factors and fluctuating levels of melatonin. *Food & Nutrition Research, 56.* https://doi.org/10.3402/fnr.v56i0.17252

Radzyminski, S., & Callister, L. C. (2016). Mother's beliefs, attitudes, and decision making related to infant feeding choices. *The Journal of Perinatal Education, 25*(1), 18–28. https://doi.org/10.1891/1058-1243.25.1.18

Raghuram, A. (2019, December 13). *Why humour is important for parents, benefits of using humour in parenting.* Parent Circle. https://www.parentcircle.com/why-humour-is-important-for-parents/article

Raising Children Network. (2020, May 18). *Introducing solids: why, when, what and how.* https://raisingchildren.net.au/babies/breastfee ding-bottle-feeding-solids/solids-drinks/introducing-solids

Raising Children Network. (2022, April 20). *Outdoor play.* https://raisingchildren.net.au/babies/play-learning/outdoor-play/outdoor-play

Raising Children Network. (2022, August 15). *Children learning to feed themselves.* https://raisingchildren.net.au/babies/breastfee ding-bottle-feeding-solids/solids-drinks/learning-to-feed-themselves

Raising Children Network (2022, December 16). *What's in a smile?* https://raisingchildren.net.au/babies/connecting-communicating/bonding/whats-in-a-smile

Raising Children Network. (2022, December 19). *Community connections for children: friends, neighbours and local organisations.* https://raisingchildren.net.au/school-age/connecting-communicating/connecting/helping-your-child-connect-with-others

Raising Children Network. (n.d.). *Newborns: health and daily care.* https://raisingchildren.net.au/newborns/health-daily-care

Santos-Longhurst, A. (2018, August 31). *High cortisol symptoms: what do they mean?* Healthline. https://www.healthline.com/health/high-cortisol-symptoms#symptoms

Schenker, S. (2021, April 27). *Bonding with your baby through shared food.* Weaning World. https://weaningworld.com/bonding-with-your-baby-through-shared-food/

Scott, S. (2015). *Why we laugh.* [Video].TED Talks. https://www.ted.com/talks/sophie_scott_why_we_laugh

Senior, J. (2014). *For parents, happiness is a very high bar.* [Video].TED Talks. https://www.ted.com/talks/jennifer_senior_fo r_parents_happiness_is_a_very_high_bar

Setterquist, H., & Garner, C. D. (n.d.). *Fish oils during pregnancy and lactation.* Infant Risk Center. https://www.infantrisk.com/content/fish-oil-supplementation-during-pregnancy-and-lactation

Seuss. (1978). *I can read with my eyes shut!.* Harper Collins.

Sparling, E. (2015, July 8). *Use your brain for a change.* Hummingbird Learning Centre. https://hummingbirdlearning.com/use-your-brain-for-a-change/

Spector, N. (2018, January 10). *Smiling can trick your brain into happiness — and boost your health.* NBC News. https://www.nbcnews.com/better/health/smili ng-can-trick-your-brain-happiness-boost-your-health-ncna822591

St-Onge, M.-P., Mikic, A., & Pietrolungo, C. E. (2016). Effects of diet on sleep quality. *Advances in Nutrition, 7*(5), 938–949. https://doi.org/10.3945/an.116.012336

Stanford Medicine Children's Health. (2019). *Infant sleep.* https://www.stanfordchildrens.org/en/topic/d efault?id=infant-sleep-90-P02237

Stanford Medicine Children's Health. (2019). *Why the family meal is important.* https://www.stanfordchildrens.org/en/topic/default?id=why-the-family-meal-is-important-1-701

Stockdale, A. (n.d.). *Six benefits of using child-led learning.* Generation Mindful. https://genmindful.com/blogs/mindful-moments/benefits-of-child-led-learning

Swanson, W. S. (2013, March 28). *Ten reasons why infants wake up at night.* Dr. Wendy Sue Swanson. https://www.wendysueswanson.com/why-do-babies-wake-up-at-night/#:~:text=Most%20babies%20wake%20up%20at

Tan, V. (2017, June 3). *How to increase the absorption of iron from foods.* Healthline Media. https://www.healthline.com/nutrition/increase-iron-absorption

Tasnim, N., Quin, C., Gill, S., Dai, C., Hart, M., & Gibson, D. L. (2021). Early life environmental exposures have a minor impact on the gut ecosystem following a natural birth. *Gut Microbes, 13*(1). https://doi.org/10.1080/19490976.2021.1875797

Taylor, M. (2020, October 12). *Why is my toddler suddenly waking up overnight?* What to Expect.

https://www.whattoexpect.com/toddler/behavior/night-waking.aspx

Tham, E., Schneider, N., & Broekman, B. (2017). Infant sleep and its relation with cognition and growth: A narrative review. *Nature and Science of Sleep, 9*, 135–149. https://doi.org/10.2147/nss.s125992

The Parent Practice. (2020, August 10). *Eighty percent of parenting is modelling.* https://www.theparentpractice.com/blog/80-of-parenting-is-modelling

Tucker, F. (2014, November 14). *What is autonomy and why does it matter?* IFamily. https://www.ifamilystudy.eu/what-is-autonomy-and-why-does-it-matter/

Ungar, T. (2017). Neuroscience, Joy, and the Well-Infant Visit That Got Me Thinking. *Annals of Family Medicine, 15*(1), 80–83. https://doi.org/10.1370/afm.2013

UNICEF. (2013). *The first 1,000 days of life: The brain's window of opportunity.* https://www.unicef-irc.org/article/958-the-first-1000-days-of-life-the-brains-window-of-opportunity.html

Vecht, R. (2017). *Top ten parenting tips to get the best out of your child.* LinkedIn. https://www.linkedin.com/pulse/top-10-

parenting-tips-get-best-out-your-child-rachel-vecht

Wallis, N. (2020, November 27). *Why the first 1,000 days are most important for your child's development.* nib Health Insurance. https://www.nib.co.nz/free-resources/article/nathan-wallis-why-the-first-1-000-days-are-most-important-for-your-childs/

Wassef, A., Nguyen, Q. D., & St-André, M. (2018). Anaemia and depletion of iron stores as risk factors for postpartum depression: a literature review. *Journal of Psychosomatic Obstetrics & Gynecology,* 40(1), 19–28. https://doi.org/10.1080/0167482x.2018.1427725

Weir, K. (2014). The lasting impact of neglect. *American Psychological Association,* 45(6). https://www.apa.org/monitor/2014/06/neglect

Worley, S. L. (2018). The extraordinary importance of sleep: The detrimental effects of inadequate sleep on health and public safety drive an explosion of Sleep research. *P & T : A Peer-Reviewed Journal for Formulary Management, 43*(12), 758–763. https://www.ncbi.nlm.nih.gov/pmc/articles/PMC6281147/

Yüksel, O., Ateş, M., Kızıldağ, S., Yüce, Z., Koç, B., Kandiş, S., Güvendi, G., Karakılıç, A., Gümüş,

H., & Uysal, N. (2019). Regular aerobic voluntary exercise increased oxytocin in female mice: The cause of decreased anxiety and increased empathy-like behaviors. *Balkan Medical Journal, 36*(5), 257–262. https://doi.org/10.4274/balkanmedj.galenos.2019.2018.12.87

Printed in Great Britain
by Amazon